A Fine-Spotted Trout on Corral Creek:

On the Cutthroat Competition
of Native Trout in the Northern Rockies

To the Reader

Annually, over three million people visit Glacier National Park. Private donations help to fill in the gap between the needs of the park and dwindling federal funding.

Glacier National Park Conservancy is the park's official fundraising nonprofit partner. GNPC supports important research, education, and wilderness preservation projects. Its mission assures that the park will remain a national treasure for generations to come.

Visit glacier.org to learn more about the Conservancy.

All royalties earned from the sale of *A Fine-Spotted Trout on Corral Creek* will be matched by the publisher and donated to the Glacier National Park Conservancy.

A Fine-Spotted Trout
on Corral Creek:

On the Cutthroat Competition
of Native Trout in the Northern Rockies

Matthew Dickerson

Heartstreams Series, Vol. III

San Antonio, Texas

2021

First Edition
ISBN: 978-1-60940-617-2

E-books:
ISBN: 978-1-60940-618-9

Wings Press
P.O. Box 591176
San Antonio, Texas 78259

Wings Press books are distributed to the trade by
Independent Publishers Group
www.ipgbook.com

Due to the 2020 pandemic, no Library of Congress
cataloging-in-publication data was available.

Video essays related to the written narrative essays in this book may be viewed at the Trout Downstream and Heart Streams YouTube channel through the playlist "Wild and Native Cutthroat Trout": www.youtube.com/playlist?list=PLmBeEX5ze8prdtENoPRqT7P6G24 Wt8Q9J.

Contents

I have been hardly more than a wandering explorer (or trespasser) in the land, full of wonder but not of information.

— J.R.R. Tolkien
"On Fairy-Stories"

In a way, people learn best when information enters through their peripheral vision, out of the corner of their eye, not viewed directly head-on, but through stories.... Native trout can return to their streams only when people view their existence as essential to their lives. And this can only happen if we see and touch these amazing creatures for ourselves.

— Kurt Fausch
For the Love or Rivers:
A Scientist's Journey

Prologue:
A Wandering Explorer
and a Short Primer on Cutthroat

This book is about cutthroat trout, a "biological icon of the western United States"[1] known by the scientific classification *Oncorhynchus clarkii*. More particularly, it is about the native cutthroat trout inhabiting the Rocky Mountains of Montana and Wyoming. It is also about the places where they live, especially the national parks and national forests where they have been afforded a measure of conservation, preservation, and even restoration found in few other places on the continent. The essays are set mostly in Glacier National Park and Flathead National Forest in Montana, and in Yellowstone National Park, Bridger-Teton National Forest, and Shoshone National Forest in Wyoming. Because of these specific locations, the most important characters in the stories are Westslope cutthroat trout (*O. c. lewisii*), Yellowstone cutthroat trout (*O. c. bouvierii*), and Snake River Fine-Spotted cutthroat trout (*O.c.behnkei*), though Colorado River cutthroat (*O. c. pleuriticus*) also make a cameo appearance as do a native species of char (*Salvelinus*) commonly known as bull trout (*S. confluentus*). Many non-native trout also make appearances, but that's usually not a good thing, as we will see.

---

1 Jessica Metcalf, et al. "Historical stocking data and 19th century DNA reveal human-induced changes to native diversity and distribution of cutthroat trout" in *Molecular Ecology* 2012. *http://ppctu.org/wp-content/uploads/2015/11/mec12028_Metcalf_etal_2012.pdf* accessed 1/18/2020.

In some locales, such as Yellowstone Lake, cutthroat trout are not just protagonists of these stories; they are characters of a much grander narrative: a keystone species around which whole ecosystems have co-evolved.

I might have placed a book about cutthroat trout in a different part of the continent, and told stories about Rio Grande or Greenback cutthroat in the southern Rockies, or Bonneville or Lahontan cutthroat in the watershed of Utah's Great Basin. I might have told stories about Bear Lake or Paiute or Humboldt cutthroat. I might even have written about diadromous Coastal cutthroat in the Pacific northwest. Those stories would have been different in many ways, but similar in others. Stories about native cutthroat trout could be set over a large portion of the United States and Canada with similar themes weaving through them. It is believed that at one time, cutthroat were the second most widely distributed species of salmonid in North America—second only to lake trout (another species of char, like the bull trout). One now-extinct strain of cutthroat trout, the Lahontan cutthroat of Nevada's Pyramid Lake, was likely the largest native trout on the continent.[2]

Several rivers are also important characters in these narratives. And since the rivers are characters, so also are the lakes the rivers flow into and out of, as well as the forests, mountains, beaver ponds, and alpine meadows through which they flow. Fisheries biologist Kurt Fausch, in his enjoyable and fascinating book *For the Love of Rivers: A Scientist's Journey*, makes this ecological point clearly and succinctly: "Everything is connected." He goes on to explain: "One can no more understand a landscape by focusing only on one part than one can appreciate a landscape painting by

2   Robert J. Behnke, *Trout and Salmon of North America* (New York: The Free Press, 2002), 143-4.

viewing a few glimpses through holes in a curtain draped over it. No one part can be understood fully without considering the connections to other parts, to place it in the appropriate context within the whole landscape."[3] Though the metaphor may have a valuable literal meaning, Fausch isn't primarily giving a lesson on art, but rather making an important point about rivers and ecology:

> And so it is with "riverscapes," a term we and other scientists have used to highlight similar hierarchies and connections within streams and between streams and their riparian forests and grasslands. Just as for landscapes, understanding riverscapes requires a continuous view of rivers to learn how features at larger spatial scales such as the geology and topography along entire river segments set the context for those at the smaller scales like riffles and pools.[4]

Although, as an angler, my thoughts are eventually drawn to the riffles and pools, I should point out that to understand a riverscape with a "continuous view" one needs to include the *terrestrial* landscapes through which the river flows in addition to the larger fluvial scale of entire river segments. Riverscapes and landscapes—the aquatic and the terrestrial—are intimately intertwined, just as lacustrine and fluvial ecologies are, and even marine ecosystems and freshwater ecosystems. What happens in the forest dramatically impacts the streams that flow through the forest (even many miles away), and what happens in the river impacts the forest through which it flows (even many miles away). Fausch's book does a wonderful job explaining and elucidating those connections, especially between forest and stream.

3 Kurt D. Fausch, *For the Love of Rivers: A Scientists Journey* (Corvallis: Oregon State University Press, 2015), 51.
4 Ibid.

All of this is just another way of saying, again, that "everything is connected"; we all live downstream of one another. Even those who live upriver, also metaphorically live downstream (as the following narratives about cutthroat trout hopefully make clear); since trout swim upstream, often traveling great distances to spawn or colonize new water, whatever impacts a river (and its native fish) in one location can have repercussions a long distance away both upriver and down, and that impact can carry deep into surrounding forests. The researching and writing of this book helped bring that truth home to me in new—and at times sobering—ways.

Other characters in this story include several fisheries biologists who study and care about cutthroat trout and other native fish, and the places those fish make their homes. I have had the privilege not only of reading, learning from, and teaching from Fausch's excellent book mentioned above, but also of spending time with the man himself—including time on a little native cutthroat trout stream wandering through an alpine meadow in a national forest in the Rocky Mountains of his home state of Colorado, I with my fly rod and Kurt with his Tenkara rod, and both of us with very small flies. My understanding of cutthroat trout and their habitat has also been informed by spending time with National Park Service biologist Christopher Downs in Glacier National Park and USGS biologist Clint Muhlfeld in Glacier National Park and Flathead National Forests, and by reading their important scientific studies. And further south in Wyoming, I enjoyed and benefited from spending time traipsing through the Shoshone National Forest with USFS biologist Shawn Anderson discussing the protection and restoration of native trout, and also interviewing USFS biologist Matt Anderson (who at the time was stationed in Bridger-Teton National Forest) about a project to restore native Colorado

River cutthroat to a headwater tributary of the Colorado.

Of course, I also am a character in these stories—not a very important one, but the one whose narrative voice tells the stories of the other more important characters. In playing the role of narrator, I think of the words of author J.R.R.Tolkien at the start of one of his famous essays: "And overbold I may be accounted, for though I have been a lover of fairy-stories since I learned to read and have at times thought about them, I have not studied them professionally. I have been hardly more than a wandering explorer (or trespasser) in the land, full of wonder but not of information."[5]

I come to cutthroat trout and the waters where they live full of wonder: wonder in the sense of curiosity, delight, and awe all rolled into one. But I cannot claim to have professionally studied them, at least not as a professional scientist in the way that Fausch, Downs, Muhlfeld, Anderson or Anderson have. To continue stealing from Tolkien's words, I have been a wandering explorer in the world where cutthroat live. At times—particularly when I am involved in the intricate dance that some call "playing" and others call "fighting," in which I and the cutthroat are at opposite ends of the same line, one trying to continue the dance and the other trying to break it off—I have felt like an overbold trespasser, or perhaps a voyeur. But like many dancers, I am also a lover, of both the cutthroat trout and the places they live. I have been so since I first made their acquaintance some forty-plus years ago. And scientific study, although tremendously valuable, is not the only way to know something or to communicate that knowledge; it is neither the sole way to be filled with information nor the only type of information that is valuable. Fausch (himself a scientist who does a wonderful job telling

---

5 J.R.R.Tolkien, "On Fairy-Stories" in *Tree and Leaf* (Boston: Houghton Mifflin Company, 1989), 9.

personal stories in addition to and as a means toward conveying scientific data) notes in his book: "In a way, people learn best when information enters through their peripheral vision, out of the corner of their eye, not viewed directly head-on, but through stories."[6] Some of the best stories, the ones that impact us most deeply, are ones we get to live out. Thus later in his book Fausch adds, "Native trout can return to their streams only when people view their existence as essential to their lives. And this can only happen if we see and touch these amazing creatures for ourselves."[7]

Robin Wall Kimmerer (another scientist who is also a wonderful writer) in her book *Braiding Sweetgrass* makes yet another point about needing the eyes of a poet as well as those of a scientist—and about learning from both the native tradition of her ancestors and from the scientific tradition she was trained to in the university. "When I stare too long at the world with science eyes," she notes, "I see an afterimage of traditional knowledge." She then asks an important question, drawing on her own metaphor of how the beauty of goldenrod and asters is magnified when they grow close together and are seen in contrast. "Might science and traditional knowledge be purple and yellow to one another, might they be goldenrod and asters? We see the world more fully when we use both." She then points out, "When botanists go walking the forests and fields looking for plants, we say we are going on a foray. When writers do the same, we should call it a metaphoray, and the land is rich in both. We need them both."[8]

So I am not ashamed to admit that—as much as I have benefited from the knowledge gained from the professional

---

6 Fausch, *For the Love of Rivers*, 127.
7 Ibid., 181-2.
8 Kimmerer, *Braiding Sweetgrass*, 46.

scientists, both through their writings and through personal interactions—my favorite way to get to know the piscine characters in these stories has been spending time with them in their homes where they eat and live out their lives. I love to sit by a quiet stream (or a loud river, for that matter), listening, watching, breathing, smelling, and being attentive and present: watching the osprey hover sixty feet above the water before plunging straight downward, or the graceful and stealthy blue heron quietly stalking the shoreline, both birds seeking the same sort of prey I seek, though with methods that differ greatly from each other and from me; listening to the sough of wind through the branches overheard, the rumbling of the cascades, or the constant rolling of gravel down the stream bottom between my wadered feet—or the buzz of the mosquito in my ear, or louder drone of its thousand cousins in streamside brush; pausing as an unaware whitetail takes a drink from the stream thirty yards away, or an elk wanders the hillside above; admiring the incomparably delicate wings of some *emphemeroptera* rising from the water for the first time, or for the last time landing back upon its surface with translucent wings, its life spent in the acting of beginning another generation of lives; marveling at the casing of a caddis fly, who—like the beaver that built the dam three hundred yards upriver—spins its home with whatever material is at hand.

And, ultimately, I am drawn to the dance itself, delighting even when I fail to find a dance partner, or when in a breathless moment the partner accepts my invitation only to leave me seconds letter, and my heart races as I find myself having once again executed a long-distance release. Indeed, I especially delight in the dance, however short or long-lived the dance is—a dance to a soundtrack that temporarily fades into the background once the dance begins. I delight in the moment I wait for when I and my dance partner come together briefly at the end.

I met my first cutthroat trout just over forty years before writing this book, in the mid-1970s, when my father's work took our family from New England to Colorado and New Mexico for a month in the middle of the summer. At the time, I knew little to nothing about the distinctions between different genera of trout—between *Oncorhynchus, Salvelinus,* or *Salmo.* I didn't know which were native to the Rockies (or to which parts of the Rockies), and even if I had I wouldn't have known why it was important. I was equally happy catching rainbow trout, brook trout, or cut-bows as I was catching a real cutthroat.

Half a decade later, my brother moved to Boulder for college, and between his undergraduate work, marriage to a Coloradan, starting a family, graduate school, and work, he spent considerable time over the next two decades living a mile above sea level at the eastern edge of the Rocky Mountains. We had many adventures together, most of which involved chasing trout in the mountains. We backpacked up a steep mountain slope high above the timberline and survived a thundrous hail storm out in the open, on the edge of a glacier near the continental divide, so that we could fish a little tarn for eight-inch cutthroat that fed for only thirty minutes in the morning and thirty minutes in the evening on tiny midges. And we fished some big famous rivers also, catching mostly non-native rainbows and browns.

When my uncle homesteaded in northern British Columbia, I was able to visit him twice, once in high school and again the year I graduated from college. I caught brightly colored coastal cutthroat out of the log-jammed beaver pond in his yard fed by a cold stream that flowed off the steep mountain behind his house. And when I felt bolder, I crossed the railroad tracks and caught bigger cutthroat trout huddled against the rocky shoreline of the Skeena River. On the drive back from my uncle's, I spent an evening hiking into a remote pond in Jasper National Park for some fly fishing, unsuccessful in the sense that I saw no trout, but successful in every other way. A few days later I redeemed the lack of success in Jasper with an amazing afternoon hiking into a remote lake in Banff National Park where cutthroat eagerly took little artificial dry flies. So inspired was I by the beauty of the place, and by the abundance of wild cutthroat, that I returned two years later for an extended backpacking trip to fish more of Banff's backcountry lakes—in one of which I ended up catching not cutthroat trout, but non-native rainbows and brook trout.

Yet for all of those delightful and formative experiences (and many others I have not mentioned) it was not until the summer of 2012 and then especially in the summers of 2016 and 2017 that I really began intentionally to learn about the ways of cutthroat trout, not merely as a beautiful game species to pursue with a fly in the midst of breathtaking landscapes—a species that to some anglers seemed interchangeable with or even inferior to brook, brown, and rainbow trout—but as a native fish of vital historical and ecological significance to the places where they dwelt.

In August of 2012, my friend David O'Hara and I were given a collaborative environmental writing residency for two weeks at a cabin on Oregon's Shotpouch Creek through Oregon State University's Spring Creek Project. Ironically, we spent our time in a cabin on a little cutthroat trout stream on the west coast, finishing our book about native brook trout in the Appalachian Mountains on the east coast.[9] But every day I went out and spent time exploring Shotpouch Creek. Sometimes we just walked along or sat looking at the streamside trees, flowers, and other plants, and observing the abundant insect life especially of aquatic macroinvertebrates. On some occasions, I explored with a fly rod making brief acquaintance with the stream's little native cutthroat, which rarely grew longer than eight inches.

One of these cutthroat lived in a pool just a hop and a jump from the corner of the deck of our cabin. I named her Carol, and watched her every day from the top of the bank, as she slowly inspired an essay about her and her home.[10]

Four years later, I devoted much of the summer of 2016 to learning and writing about the native cutthroat trout of Wyoming. Accompanied by two undergraduate research assistants from Middlebury College, Julia Kendrick and Yuki Hu, I spent July in the Bridger-Teton National Forest, Yellowstone National Park, the northern district of the Shoshone National Forest, and the Popo Agie Wilderness area in the Wind River Range in the southern district of the Shoshone National Forest. We observed. We interviewed biologists (and also a well-known fishing guide), visited native fish restoration projects, and stopped into a state fish hatchery that raised native fish stock to reintroduce into the wild. We filmed trout from under and above

---

9 David O'Hara and Matthew Dickerson, *Downstream: Reflections on Brook Trout, Fly Fishing, and the Waters of Appalachia*, (Eugene: Cascade Press, 2014).
10 "The Clearcut, the Cutthroat, and the Cascade Effect", *The Written River* 5:2 (Winter, 2015) 6-9. Reprinted in *Books and Culture* (June, 2015). Reprinted in *The Few Reader* edited by Amanda Memoli et al. (Colorado State University: Fountainhead Press, 2018) 383-391.

the water. We also camped in the wilderness and in USFS cabins and sought as best as possible to experience place and not mere space. We spent the last day of the trip in Colorado with Kurt Fausch on a little wild cutthroat stream in a national forest. And in almost all the places we visited (except the hatchery, of course), I used my fly rod and flies to find more than a few trout and learn where they lived and when and what they ate.[11]

I'm sad to say that we encountered more non-native fish than native fish on that trip. We caught non-native rainbow trout in the North Fork of the Shoshone River and non-native brook trout as well as various varieties of rainbow-cutthroat hybrids up at 10,000-foot elevations on the South Fork of the Little Wind River in the Popo-Agie Wilderness. We never found a native Colorado River cutthroat in Bridger-Teton on La Barge Creek despite the ongoing effort to restore them and their habitat there (though we did find a couple of them in Colorado with Kurt Fausch at the very end of the trip). However one of the most memorable experiences of the summer was spending time on Corral Creek, a tumbling, meandering little feeder creek to Greys River where I found several beautifully and distinctively colored and patterned Snake-River Fine-Spotted cutthroat. One state fisheries biologist assured me that the Corral Creek fish were native and wild, with no evidence of historic impact of non-native stocking.

In the summer of 2017 my study of native cutthroat of the northern Rockies continued, this time with West-slope cutthroat—a species whose scientific name honors

---

11 The video series on "Wild and Native Cutthroat Trout", based on the author's experiences in the national forests and national parks of Wyoming and Montana, can be found on YouTube at https://www.youtube. com/playlist?list=PLmBeEX5ze8prdtENoPRqT7P6G24Wt8Q9J.

both named leaders of the famous Lewis and Clark Expedition—when I was chosen to be Artist-in-Residence at Glacier National Park for the month of June. Time with biologists Downs and Muhlfeld proved greatly informative, providing both sobering news and hope, and most especially more insights into why native cutthroat are so important, and are not simply replaceable by some other trout such as rainbows or eastern brook trout. (Some of the stories of that summer appeared in my book *The Voices of Rivers*.)

So what did I learn? The only real way to share that answer is through the stories that follow. However, for readers less familiar with cutthroat trout—the history of the species, its many strains and subspecies, the diversity even within the same subspecies, its past and present geographic distribution, and the threats the species continues to face in its native habitat—I conclude this introduction with a quick primer culled from the works of the scientists mentioned above and especially from Robert Behnke's' classic text, *Trout and Salmon of North America*.[12]

Around 2.5 million years ago, the species that would become cutthroat trout were evolving in the Columbia River Basin. They most likely diverged from rainbow trout (*Oncorhynchus mykiss*) between two and one million years ago, with cutthroat becoming the more genetically complex species, having 64 to 68 chromosomes compared with 58 to 60 found in most populations of rainbow trout. As the cut-

---

12　For the following discussion, see Behnke pages 18 and 139-148; Fausch starting at p. 158; Loxterman and Keeley "Watershed boundaries and geographic isolation: patterns of diversification in cutthroat trout from western North America" in *Evolutionary Biology* 2012, **12:38**; and also Metcalf et al, "Historical stocking data and 19th century DNA reveal human-induced changes to native diversity and distribution of cutthroat trout" in *Molecular Ecology* 2012.

throat colonized the Pacific northwest and the watershed of the Columbia River, the various populations became geographically isolated. Evidence suggests that by about one million years ago, the cutthroat species had already formed into four different evolutionary branches even as they continued to colonize and become more isolated. It wasn't until very recently in geologic time—possibly within the past 10,000 years (toward the end of the previous ice age), or even as recently as 6,000 years ago—that colonizing cutthroat were able to get across watershed divides. Perhaps making use of some little beaver pond or tarn straddling the Continental Divide, they made it from the west slope of the Rocky Mountains and the Pacific watershed onto the east slope, including both the Missouri River headwaters flowing into the Gulf of Mexico and the Saskatchewan River watershed that flows northeastward into the Hudson Bay and the Arctic Ocean. At some point they also successfully crossed other watershed divides heading south down into Utah's Great Basin and into another Pacific drainage, the Colorado River. Once in these watersheds, they were able to climb back up numerous other tributaries, once again reaching higher elevation streams until impassable barriers halted their progress. By the time Europeans began exploring the continent, some subspecies of cutthroat trout was present from southern New Mexico all the way up to Alaska's Kenai Peninsula, and from the Pacific Coast inland all the way to the east slope of the Rockies in the eastern half of Colorado as well as the Yellowstone River and much of the width of Montana.

Geographic isolation also meant that the various subspecies of cutthroat evolved different traits adapted to their different environments, including significant differences in coloration and patterns as well as diet. Some of the traits were even micro-adaptations within the same subspecies resulting from slight differences in climate, water flow, and ideal spawning times from others in neighboring watersheds. The Snake River Fine-Spotted cutthroat trout (named after Robert Behnke) that lives in the Greys River watershed of the Bridger-Teton National Forest on the west slope of the Rockies in western Wyoming is closely related to and in the same evolutionary family as the more famous Yellowstone subspecies that inhabits waters on the eastern slope including its namesake lake and numerous tributaries in the national park. As of very recently, genetic markers could not distinguish the two strains, and thus some scientists do not even acknowledge the Snake River Fine-Spotted to be a distinct subspecies. And yet they have distinctly different patterning and coloration, which is clearly a genetic trait as each will reproduce after its kind. Likewise, the Westslope cutthroat native to Glacier National Park and Montana's Flathead National Forest also has its own distinct coloration and adaptations, including a diet that eschews smaller forage fish in favorite of aquatic macro-invertebrates—a diet very unlike that Lahontan cutthroat that grew to enormous sizes by being piscivorous.

The diversity within the species also includes a diversity of life histories, even within the same subspecies or population. The Pacific northwest boasts a population of semi-anadromous (also called diadromous) Coastal cutthroat that—while not truly anadromous like a Pacific salmon that spends years at sea before spawning—will move back and forth between salt water and fresh, spending three months or so at a time in a marine environment. Some cutthroat are adfluvial, living much of their adult lives in lakes, but leaving the lakes to spawn in rivers and streams. Even among the adfluvial strains of Westslope cutthroat trout in Montana's national parks and forests, some genetic strains have adapted to be outlet spawners and some are inlet spawners. Other cutthroat trout are purely fluvial, living their entire lives in running water. Among these some have adapted to small streams and others to large rivers. And while nearly all cutthroat (like most other species of trout) spawn in running water, with a particular preference for small cold headwater streams, the species even has some strains with fully lacustrine life histories, spawning on shoals in lakes that have a particularly good oxygen supply. This tremendous diversity in the gene pool that exists even within geographically overlapping populations of the same subspecies provides extra resilience; an environmental catastrophe that impacts one subpopulation may leave other subpopulations largely unaffected.

There has been some ongoing debate and occasional confusion about classification and early distribution of subspecies of cutthroat trout. What cutthroat trout specialists do not need to debate is that there are numerous environmental threats to the species. Many of these threats have already had devastating effects. As Behnke notes, "The species' present distribution and abundance is only a small fraction of what it was before the impacts of western settlement, and two of 14 subspecies are extinct."[13] And Fausch adds, "It is among the great tragedies of the West that these fish are now gone from most of our rivers."[14] The threats could be divided into four broad categories: habitat degradation or loss, climate change, river fragmentation, and invasive species. Each of these could be further divided.

Habitat loss is often the most visible threat, at least to local populations of cutthroat. It comes as result of resource extraction (forestry and mining), development including

13 Behnke, 147.
14 Fausch, 161.

road-building, and also degradation from activities such as agriculture, grazing, or water withdrawal. Fausch gives a good summary of examples and the damage each causes. Mining operations "funneled large amounts of sand and silt into streams that clogged spawning gravel", with sediment that at times "carried heavy metals like cadmium and zinc that are highly toxic to fish eggs and larvae." Logging operations destroyed stream beds and riparian canopy, and resulted in further siltation and stream warming. "Overgrazing and trampling of stream banks by free-ranging cattle also brought sediment into streams that clogged gravels and filled pools." And, as Fausch also notes, water withdrawal for irrigation (or drinking and bathing in larger cities) could leave sections of stream beds nearly dried up.[15] Each of these is a stressor. Even when native fish populations are resilient to some stressors, the accumulation of them makes populations less resilient and can lead to collapse.

Climate change could be added to the category of habitat loss, but it probably deserves its own category. Trout are cold water fish. Warming water alone isn't necessarily a problem; in many places where cutthroat have been displaced—either by non-native species or from habitat degradation—they have been pushed further upriver toward high elevation streams that are actually colder than their ideal temperatures. Some warming of water in and of itself might not negatively impact these populations. However climate change has many other devastating impacts beyond raising water temperatures. It can alter conditions for spawning or have many other indirect consequences by (for example) changing tree species or opening the path for more invasive species. Indeed, the problems can run much deeper. Climate change is resulting in the loss of glaciers and annual snow packs which

15 Fausch, 162.

are needed to provide summertime flows of cold water, and is likely at least partially responsible for the burning of forests, and the increase in catastrophic storms. All of these are additional stressors. In the case of the loss of glaciers, the stressor can be dramatic.

River fragmentation is a more complex issue than habitat loss, although it often results in lost or degraded habitat. River fragmentation is the result of artificial barriers such as dams or (on smaller streams) culverts, which prevent the passage of fish upstream. Even when such a dam leaves some quality habitat on both the upstream and downstream side, it can have negative consequences.

In the extreme case where access to spawning waters is blocked by a dam or other barrier, the result can be the extirpation. Behnke suggests that "blockage of spawning tributaries" was one of the factors in extirpating native cutthroat from Lake Tahoe.[16] Even in less extreme cases, fragmentation can harm the resilience of a fish population. Over the course of their lives, cutthroat trout need access to a variety of habitats: spawning habitat of shallow gravelly well-oxygenated riffles, deeper pools for overwintering, and food-rich summer feeding locations. A trout population in a fragmented river with access to good spawning habitat, but without overwintering pools, may not survive. When a river is excessively fragmented, then even a population of fish with enough water to survive from generation to generation is genetically cut off from others of its species which can result in less resilience.

---

16 Behnke, 144.

Despite how harmful all three of the previous environmental threats have proven, the biologists with whom I spoke were all of the opinion that invasive fish have been the greatest historic cause of the decline of cutthroat and remain the most significant threat. As Behnke notes at the start of his section on cutthroat conservation: "The cutthroat trout is highly sensitive to environmental changes, *especially the introduction of nonnative species or trout*" (emphasis added). Without diminishing the impacts of the other factors, a paragraph later he repeats his message. "Cutthroat trout are very sensitive to changes in water quality, especially increases in sediment and water temperature resulting from logging, road building, and livestock grazing. The greatest negative impact, however, has been introductions of nonnative trout, especially rainbow trout, with which cutthroat trout hybridize."[17]

In the places I visited in Montana and Wyoming, the three non-native species particularly damaging to populations of cutthroat trout are all human-introduced trout stocked for recreational purposes: rainbow trout, brook trout, and lake trout. In many higher elevation streams and lakes, brook trout overpopulate, outcompete, and displace the native cutthroat, often pushing them up into higher and more marginal habitats—or eradicating them altogether. I visited some high elevation streams in the Wind River Range in the southern district of the Shoshone National Forest where the brook trout were so thick that the streams looked like hatchery raceways. In the cutthroat competition between the native fish and the invaders, which has repeatedly played out over the past century and a half across countless Rocky Mountain waters, the native cutthroat has usually lost.

Lake trout have proven even more deadly in some plac-

17 Behnke, 147.

es. As large piscivores, they prey upon cutthroat, feasting on them in great quantities. In the famous Yellowstone Lake, lake trout have decimated the native cutthroat population with devastating effects cascading throughout the whole ecosystem to impact cutthroat-dependent species such as osprey, grizzly bears, and pelicans. Introduction of lake trout to Lake Tahoe, combined with the blockage of spawning streams mentioned earlier, contributed to the extirpation of cutthroat in that water. If the ongoing intervention and efforts to suppress lake trout in Yellowstone Lake ceases, it might end up with the same fate as Lake Tahoe.

Yet the impact of invasive rainbow trout is even more devastating than the cutthroat competition of the brook trout, or the predation by lake trout. Oddly, the problem is not rainbow trout eating cutthroat fingerlings or competing with them for food (though some of both of those may happen in some waters), but rather the hybridization of rainbow trout with native cutthroat. Hybridization results in the very end of the species as a species (even if some of the native genes persist in hybridized form.) "Once hybridization begins," Behnke notes, "the native cutthroat population is lost."[18]

USGS fisheries biologist Clint Muhlfeld made the point to me repeatedly when I spent a day with him in Glacier National Park and Flathead National Forest, on a research and teaching trip studying bull trout and Westslope cutthroat (in June of 2017): when the native genes of cutthroat are replaced in the ecosystem (through stocking and hybridization) with genes of hatchery rainbow trout, the genetic diversity of the native fish and the corresponding fitness, resilience, and adaptability get lost.

"What measures of fitness?" I asked Clint.

---

18   Behnke, 141.

"All of them," he answered.

Of course this is all mere information about cutthroat trout, learned from books and the mouths of scientists because I was curious, or because I was fortunate to be in the right place at the right time. (And the last few paragraphs have been rather dismal bits of information.) It was through experience and story that this information became much more real—that I even had some of the right questions to

ask, or at least the right frame of mind to be attentive to the answers.

Robin Wall Kimmerer, even while doing the important work of science, makes an important point about the value of listening, and being present. It is a point I relate to, and which is perhaps behind much of the point of this book.

> Listening in wild places, we are audience to conversations in a language not our own. I think now that it was a longing to comprehend this language I hear in the woods that led me to science, to learn over the years to speak fluent botany. . . . To name and describe you must first see, and science polishes the gift of seeing. I honor the strength of that language that has become a second tongue to me. But beneath the richness of its vocabulary and descriptive power, something is missing, that same something that swells around you and in you when you listen to the world.[19]

So even as I seek to be informed by scientific study, so I seek even more to be informed and shaped by listening.

---

19 Kimmerer, 48-49.

One of the wonderful aspects of her book *Pilgrim at Tinker Creek*—an aspect suggested in the title—is that the author Annie Dillard really does come to her experiences as a pilgrim on a journey to discover: a very attentive pilgrim ready to be captured by awe. She is a pilgrim very much like the wandering explorer Tolkien claimed to be, embarking on the pilgrimage not (yet) full of information, but very much full of wonder. Or, perhaps more accurately, Dillard comes full of a willingness to find wonder. "Our life is a faint tracing on the surface of mystery,"[20] she writes. And a little later she adds to that reflection:

> I've been thinking about seeing. There are lots of things to see, unwrapped gifts and free surprises. The world is fairly studded and strewn with pennies cast broadside from a generous hand. But—and this is the point—who gets excited by a mere penny? If you follow one arrow, if you crouch motionless on a bank to watch a tremulous ripple thrill on the water and are rewarded by the sight of a muskrat kit paddling from its den, will you count that sight a chip of copper only, and go your rueful way? It is dire poverty indeed when a man is so malnourished and fatigued that he won't stoop to pick up a penny. But if you cultivate a healthy poverty and simplicity, so that finding a penny will literally make your day, then, since the world is in fact planted with pennies, you have with your poverty bought a lifetime of days.[21]

Dillard's wisdom is one the earth needs. So I come to world of cutthroat trout also as a poor man—though with what I hope is a "healthy poverty and simplicity", looking to pick up some pennies.

---

20 Annie Dillard, *Pilgrim at Tinker Creek*, in *Three by Annie Dillard* (New York: HarperPerennial, 1990) 16.
21 Dillard, 21-22.

I.

A Fine-Spotted Cutthroat on Corral Creek
(and an Impassable Barrier)

Bridger-Teton National Forest, July 2016

Although the sky won't fade to pink for two more hours, the sun has already dropped behind the long ridgeline of the Salt River Mountains behind me. The shadows of these 10,000-foot peaks stretch over me, engulfing the river valley, leaving only the mountaintops and highest ridges of the Wyoming Range to the east still bathed in evening light. After another hot, dry, mid-July day, the shadows and cool evening breeze feel wonderfully refreshing. My two tired students have abandoned me for the evening, but it's not a bad place to be alone with a fly rod and a can of bear spray the final night of my visit to the Bridger-Teton National Forest.

Though I pause now and then to delight in the grandeur of the surrounding scene—admiring the peaks, breathing the scent of wild grasses, pine, and wet dirt, and also keeping a lookout for wandering bears—my attention is mostly fixed on Corral Creek. Not much wider in most places than my fly rod is long, it flows gently over a shallow riffle past my feet and on toward a long pool beside steep undercut banks where it bends to the left. The deep part of the pool looks like it would drop me to my armpits if I tried to wade it. Though the bushes are too tall to see around the bend from where I stand, I know beyond this bend the stream passes through another trio of deep holes surrounded by a tangle of brush, then takes another sharp bend back to the right and plunges its final hundred yards down a steeper gradient to its confluence with Greys River.

Where the riffle meets the pool, a steady succession of delicate, sulfur-colored *ephemeroptera*—insects known more commonly as mayflies—emerge from the stream and take to flight in search of a mate. I also catch an occasional glimpse of grasshoppers, crawling and jumping through the tall grasses beside the stream. Surely now and then one must stay aloft too long, or perhaps not long enough, or at a bad time when the breeze huffs in from the wrong direction, and alight not in the safety of the grass but on the surface of the flowing stream. That thought crosses my mind not out of any wish to see the demise of grasshoppers, but because I am also watching a pod of cutthroat trout rising regularly in the soft water both inside the bend where the current pushes against the steep bank and also in a little protected cut right against that bank. The aggressive strikes suggests that the trout are pursuing aquatic insects as they hatch, trying to get them on the surface of the stream before they can take flight. But surely the hungry fish would be happy to grab a much bigger mouthful if a stray terrestrial insect were to fall on the water on a breezy mid-summer evening.

With that latter thought in mind, I forgo a mayfly pattern and tie on a yellow grasshopper imitation. Even with the thick brush behind me, it's an easy cast to where the fish are rising. It takes a couple tries to adjust the drift of my fly so that it doesn't drag unnaturally as it floats. I make several more casts, drifting my grasshopper pattern along various paths: the near seam, the far seam, right down the center of the current. It does not provoke even a single serious look. The fish are still rising, though. I study the rising mayflies more closely now. I don't have a fly pattern with me that matches this hatch exactly, but a #16 Adams is close in size and color. I tie one on and within the first few casts it draws their attention. I soon land and release two beautiful cutthroat, both between fifteen and sixteen inches long. In addition to the characteristic red accent below their jaws that gives them their name, they also have the distinctive small black dots of the Snake River Fine-Spotted subspecies, the native strain that inhabits this watershed.[22] I'm delighted to catch them, and to know this native fish is thriving here. Though at many times in my life I have enjoyed catching rainbow trout and brook trout, I am glad I won't find either of them on this stream.

I work my way around the bend, down to the next hole, an even deeper one. There I land a third fish on dry flies. I fish a while longer, hoping to entice the lunker I know is hiding there. Down in this deep valley, however, dusk descends quickly. The Cazier Guard Station cabin where I am staying is only a few hundred yards away, but it is over on the east side of Greys River. I don't want to wade back in complete dark. And tomorrow will be a long day of travel. I should get some sleep. I continue down Corral Creek to its confluence with Greys.

The pool at the confluence is bigger than anything on Corral Creek. It has skunked me both times I've fished it over the past two days. I have a feeling tonight will be different, though. I watch the surface for a moment in the dim

---

22 Since it is genetically indistinguishable from a Yellowstone cutthroat (*O.c.bouvieri*)—at least using current genetic techniques—some biologists speak of this cutthroat as part of the Yellowstone subspecies. Yet the fish is visibly different from other Yellowstone cutthroats in its spot pattern, and the offspring of a reproducing pair of Snake River Fine-Spotted cuts will resemble its ancestors, and so many biologists have accepted the Snake River Fine-Spotted as its own subspecies, naming it after Robert Behnke (*O.c.behnkei*).

twilight. I don't see any splashes or swirls—no sign here of trout feeding or even of the hatching mayflies. I clip off the dry fly and tie on a heavy cone-head muddler, which imitates a little sculpin or forage fish. It's too dark to see any action below the surface. I can no longer make out the river bottom even where it's only a foot and a half deep at the upper end of the pool. It would be an easy time to lose some flies on a submerged log. But I flick the fly out anyway, landing it over the deeper water. I twitch it lightly like a darting fish as the current slides it down deeper.

The fly proves to be the right choice. I land two more fat fish, one on each side of the boulder that sits in the middle of the pool. Their fine spots and characteristic cutthroat markings are dimly visible even in the dusk. Catching and releasing them is a good way to end my visit to this area. As I make use of my wading staff to feel my way back across the river in the final embers of twilight, I think back over my travels and explorations over the past week. That earlier story helps explain why I'm especially happy to have found native cutthroat in this river, and why it's even sweeter to catch the last two in this pool.

Almost a week earlier, I am driving with Julia and Yuki into the Bridger-Teton National Forest from the southeast side. Early that day, we had visited the Kemmerer Ranger Station and picked up some useful materials, information, and advice about our visit. The drive from Kemmerer is flat, hot, dry, and brown. Once we turn off the highway in La Barge, however, the way ahead grows greener, more beautiful, and less flat with each passing mile. Distant peaks become less distant. The enticing water of La Barge Creek appears on our left. The road plunges through a cut into the midst of steep green hills. Though still in Wyoming, it feels like a different world.

The winding road continues along the northern edge of the river valley up toward the headwaters of La Barge Creek. Sometimes the creek meanders over toward our side of the valley. I glance out the window at a pool close to the road just at the right moment to see a trout snatch an insect from the surface. It suddenly becomes more difficult to keep my eyes on the road. I am eager to escape the car and the hot black pavement and begin exploring the river. All that enticing water, however, is on private land behind "No Trespassing" signs. So I keep driving toward our destination. We pass from private land to BLM lands, and onward toward the eastern edge of the national forest. My heart feels lighter now, as we exchange pavement for gravel and make our way deeper into the forested hills, further from the fenced-off river.

I know from our research that the primitive forest service road follows the westward route of the old Oregon Trail along La Barge Creek toward the Tri-Basin Divide. Oddly enough, the riverside highway had been far more crowded one hundred and sixty-five summers earlier during the peak of the famed westward migration. Today we see no covered wagons—or any other vehicles—on the road. I keep my eyes open for deer, elk, antelope, or moose. We see none of those either. I am also looking for a small dam.

We make it through BLM lands, and soon after entering the Bridger-Teton National Forest I spot what I had been looking for on my left: an earthen works dam with a concrete spillway in the center spans the creek. I pull the car over for a closer look. Water plunges about eight feet over the artificial spillway into a pool below, and then rolls on down the valley back in a natural streambed. Upstream of the dam, the impounded creek forms a pond of about five acres. As I gaze across the flat surface, another fish rises on the far end.

I look back toward the dam. This, I am sure, is part of the project we had read about at the Kemmerer Ranger Station—a project I am eager to explore. It is an artificial impassable barrier: an intentional effort to fragment the river with the purpose of keeping invasive fish on the downstream side from getting up into the waters above. What population of native cutthroat trout will we find above the dam? What will the habitat be like? What macro-invertebrate life will we find—aquatic insects that might serve as trout food? Will we find invasive trout below the dam?

Although we will return later and explore this site more closely, we take a few minutes for a quick visit, making our way toward the dam across hard dry ground blanketed sparsely with knee-high grass, clusters of lavender lupines, high country sage, and prickly evergreen shrubs. A few hundred yards up the slope on either side of us, the grass gives way to dotted trees, and then to a thicker forest. I wonder if deer are watching us from the shadows, or perhaps a bear or even a cougar. Mostly I wonder about the trout. Our feet kick up dust as we find a path through the scrubby brush. As we approach the water, the ground grows softer and the grass greener.

Soon we stand atop the concrete edifice, looking straight down toward the stream below that flows out of the plunge pool and within a few dozen yards disappears into the brush. Is the barrier really impassable? I suspect it is. The biologists and engineers who designed and built it knew what they were doing. Although I could imagine a fifteen pound spawning Atlantic salmon leaping over this dam, it's much more difficult imagining a twenty-inch invasive rainbow trout getting over it. Thus it is a vital piece of a long-term effort to reestablish native Colorado River cutthroat in upper La Barge Creek within the Bridger-Teton

National Forest—a project I am both curious and hopeful about. Many biologists consider non-native rainbow trout to be the greatest threat to native cutthroat, not primarily because they outcompete with the cutthroat (as invasive brook trout do) or prey upon them (as lake trout do), but through hybridization; despite their diverging histories, rainbow trout remain genetically similar enough to cutthroat that they can and do interbreed. Once rainbow trout get into a river with cutthroat, it is only a matter of time until the genetic strain of native cutthroat trout is gone.

Restoring native cutthroat trout to a river or watershed in which invasive fish are present therefore has three or four components. First, an impassable barrier needs to be in place to prevent future incursions of non-native fish. If a natural barrier such as a high waterfall doesn't already exist, an artificial barrier must be built. Unfortunately, such high waterfalls below native cutthroat streams are not very common. In almost all cases, cutthroat colonized the water in the first place by moving upstream. Of course if cutthroat were able to do so, then unless there has been a significant change in the geology since that time, other species can also colonize. So restoring a cutthroat trout population to one of their native waters—or protecting them where such a population still exists—usually requires the construction of a manmade (i.e. artificial) barrier. Unlike so many other dams that fragment rivers and harm fish, this one has no other purpose except to block the migration of invasive fish. It is not for irrigation, or flood control, or hydro-electric generation. The irony that preventing natural fish movement can actually help protect native fish is not lost on me.

Once an impassable barrier has been built, invasive species must be removed. This is never trivial, and in large water bodies or extensive river systems it is simply impossible. In smaller rivers like La Barge Creek, however, it may often be accomplished with a mix of mechanical and chemical means, involving multiple treatments. In the case of La Barge Creek, biologists used rotenone: a chemical that that poisons the water making it impossible for fish to get oxygen. Studies suggest that rotenone breaks down quickly and has little impact on species other than fish, and that any negative collateral effects can be mitigated further through careful timing. Nonetheless, the use of rotenone is not without controversy; although in a small enough lake or river system it can be an effective way of removing most fish, it is expensive and has environment drawbacks.

The third stage (which can only take place after the completion of the first and second) is to restore the native fish. This, of course, must be done from some population of the same native subspecies. Ideally, the reintroduction comes from wild stock rather than hatchery stock. Since cutthroat trout micro-adapt to very local river systems, diets, climates, and flow regimes, the ideal solution is to find a native population in a nearby watershed that is healthy enough to allow some fish to be taken. This, however, is often not possible. On La Barge Creek, for example, the two nearby rivers in the Tri-Basin divide flow into completely different watersheds: the Great Basin to the west and the Snake River and Columbia River watersheds to the north, rather than south into the Colorado River as La Barge Creek does. They are, therefore, populated with entirely different cutthroat subspecies. So biologists work to carefully select the best possible genetic match from another drainage that holds native Colorado River cutthroat.

A fourth possible component to reintroduction, which can go on concurrently with all three stages described above and continue for many years after—a component that is as important for protecting and preserving existing wild fish populations as it is for restoring them—is restoration of habitat. Even if invasive species are removed from a river and prevented from returning, a restoration project will fail if the habitat can no longer support a self-sustaining native cutthroat population. Thus, for example, even while an artificial barrier is constructed that adds another point of fragmentation, the upriver portion can be de-fragmented and restored to wholeness by the removal of other unneeded barriers such as other dams, culverts, and poorly constructed road crossings.

Unfortunately, La Barge Creek had an earlier history of considerable habitat degradation. It's hard to know exactly the impact of 13,000 travelers and 80,000 head of livestock passing up a valley in one summer—as happened when it was part of the Oregon Trail—but it's not difficult to imagine the muddying of streams, pollution of water, and loss of riparian buffer.

Years later, when the railroads were being built across the west, a rail company erected a large camp along La Barge Creek to lumber the mountainsides for hack ties, which they floated downriver using splash dams. In addition to the erosion and siltation from deforestation and the lumbering operations, the sudden floods caused by the splash dams were also horribly damaging to the river ecosystem. Still later, road builders channeled the river and its smaller tributaries through metal culverts, and built dirt roads on top of the culverts. The culverts simultaneously blocked fish passage to spawning grounds, fragmented the river, and increased egg-killing siltation on the river-bottom.

The ongoing native fish restoration on La Barge Creek, as we had learned, involved the replacement of several old metal culverts with new crossings that restore natural river beds: either half culverts, or square concrete culverts, or bridges. Many of the replacements had already been done when we arrived, and we hoped to visit them. But at the cost of about $20,000 per culvert, the work was not immediate and many more remain to be completed. When we arrived at La Barge Creek, the restoration project was already a decade and a half old. We were warned that it had not yet been as successful as hoped, and that the cutthroat population was still low.

After a short visit to the dam, we continue north up the dirt Forest Road along the eastern side of La Barge Creek, following the old Oregon Trail deeper into the mountains. The river alternately winds through valleys thick with brush, slogs through beaver ponds, or tumbles along gravely riffs. As we drive, the ridges get steeper and higher on both sides, and the forests of conifers crawl further down the hills, closer to the road. We cross over La Barge Creek near the confluence where Indian Creek flows in from the west. Less than a mile later, guided by our USFS map, we turn left onto a smaller, less-traveled side road. The way gets even rougher within a few hundred yards. A couple minutes later, we arrive at the Scaler Guard Station, a U.S. Forest Service cabin where we will spent the next three nights along the South Fork of La Barge Creek.

The cabin is bigger than I pictured, with three little bunk rooms and a small eating area. It is nonetheless primitive. A faucet, sink and gas stove in the kitchen hint that at one time it was slightly less primitive. The water and gas stove, however, are both shut off. When we try to use the sink for washing dishes, we discover the hard way that the drain isn't connected either. The only luxuries are separate bunk rooms for my students and dim propane lanterns that provide enough light to dress by and almost enough to read by. The outhouse doesn't smell as bad as some, but it is still an outhouse.

Nonetheless, I am delighted to be here. The Scalar cabin could have been more primitive, or less primitive, and it would not have negatively impacted the experience. It wasn't the cabin that brought us here, but its surroundings. It stands tucked away a quiet side valley about half a mile up from the confluence of South La Barge Creek with the main stem. It is narrower than the valley we have been following for the last several miles, or the Greys River Valley where the Cazier cabin sits. It is also more heavily wooded, and more secluded. Though a few cattle graze along the edge of our road, we see no other signs of human life. The slope behind the cabin, to the southwest, rises up a steady but gentle gradient. Across the creek, the land rises more steeply to a high ridge line that now separates us from La Barge Creek. In the evenings we will watch mule deer graze across an open meadow partway up the slope directly across the creek. Bald eagles fly past, as well as osprey. We catch glimpses of elk and moose, and on one occasion while filming further up the road we will enjoy watching a herd of antelope pass by.

The stream is what I am most interested in, however. It is the first thing I want to check out. I am not disappointed. Standing on the back porch, I can look down a steep ten-foot slope almost straight into a pool below. It is much smaller than the creek we had been following, only shin to knee deep in most places and narrow enough to cross in four or five strides, with a soft sand and gravel bottom.

As soon as I unpack my gear, I walk down the hill and check it out from up close. It proves chillingly cold on the feet. At the end of a hot day, my stream thermometer reads only 48.5° F. Other than the numbing cold, however, it proves easy to wade in sandals and shorts. And the cold feels good on the feet in the hot summer air.

What really strikes me the most from the moment we arrive, however, is the tremendous number of aquatic macroinvertebrate life we can see both on the gravel river bottom and hatching into the air throughout the day. Mostly mayflies come off the water. Each of the three mornings we spend here, around 8:30 a.m., the *Ephemeroptera* start to come off the river in ones and twos, and then in tens and twenties, and within an hour they gather by hundreds and thousands in a column 150 feet tall in front of the cabin. It is the most impressive insect hatch I've ever seen on a stream that small.

Plenty of caddis fly larva, some small and some larger, also crawl around the river bottom in their homespun encasings. A few boast beautiful casings like little works of costume jewelry with a mix of both organic matter and tiny colored stones. In the afternoons, small tan caddis—something I might try to mimic with a size #16 elk hair imitation—cover the bushes beside the main stem of La Barge Creek. When I accidentally bump a bush, clouds of white wings flutter into the air like pollen. I can sit streamside and watch them in the shadows bounce from the branches of bushes eighteen inches over of the water down to the surface, and back, like thousands of mini yo-yos. In the late evenings, a darker brown caddis species—maybe size #12—flutters onto the picnic table where we sit eating dinner beside our cabin, no more than thirty yards from the water.

I see small golden stoneflies also—Yellow Sallies—not nearly as many as there are mayflies and caddisflies, but enough to notice them both in the air and on the streambed. I spot black stoneflies also. And midges, like I find in nearly every cold clean stream or river I've ever fished.

In other words, with such an array of potential food, plenty of canopy overhead, rocks and logs and small plunge pools for shade and shelter, the cutthroat trout ought to have been thriving in such a place. But I see no sign of fish. Over the next three days, I will stand for long stretches beside the cabin on the high bank looking down into the river watching for any rises or movement at or below the surface. Or I will head down to the main river and do the same thing there from the side of some bank or bridge. When I'm not filming or photographing or exploring with my students, I also seek evidence of cutthroat trout with the help of my fly rod. I drop a variety of flies on the small South Fork, out in the main stem of La Barge Creek below the confluence, further upriver toward the divide, and downriver near the edge of the national forest land close to the impassable barrier that keeps invasive trout from moving up into these reclaimed and restored waters.

All my attempts to find a Colorado River cutthroat in the La Barge Creek or its tributaries fail.

Despite the lack of fish our time is enjoyable and fruitful. For a couple nights, we are joined by Andrew Ackerman, an alumnus of Middlebury College and a professional filmmaker specializing in underwater videography. Not surprisingly, he has a much cooler drone than I have. He is also far more experienced in flying it, and in knowing how to get great footage. He came along to teach some filmmaking to Yuki, a young student at his alma mater, and to help her think through strategies for how to make compelling short videos.

We take a lot of video and photos of the river and of the visible signs of the restoration work that has been completed: the fish passage barrier, and several places where culverts have been replaced. We also document the work still remaining to be done, such as the many old culverts that still need to be replaced. At the latter locations, we get a good firsthand view of why the habitat restoration project is so important. The old culverts back up water into stagnant pools where it warms up. In some places where the culverts are too small for the volume of water that needs to pass through, or where they have been blocked by debris, little side streams pour over the road and fill with silt, muddying the river below. And even where they don't muddy the river or back up into stagnant pools, the culverts function as barriers to hinder migration to spawning habitat up side streams. I am excited to see the new projects and how natural the restored streambeds look.

It's strange how frustrations and disappointments can intersect with or even lead to successes. The lack of trout on the La Barge Creek—or at least the lack of any evidence of trout—disappointed me on multiple levels. Most importantly, it suggested that a worthwhile restoration project with important environmental implications wasn't working out. It also meant we weren't getting the video footage I hoped for. And, selfishly speaking, I wasn't having the delight of catching some wild trout and admiring their beauty. Yet the unfolding story remained interesting and important, even if it wasn't the story I had originally come to tell. The pressing question still to be answered was why the project had so far been less successful than hoped, even after fifteen years of work. And another related question: could anything different be done to improve the chances of success?

I awake on the morning of the last full day to find a flat tire on my rental car. My mind sputters with the implications of having a flat tire dozens of miles up remote backcountry roads (far from cell phone service) in a national forest, even as I start spinning through possible action plans. After breakfast, and a changeover to the spare, my unpleasant discovery sends me on a long errand back downriver, south and east to the little town of La Barge (which doesn't have a garage or mechanic) and then back north up state highway 189 to the town of Big Piney. At 10:10 a.m., I find Williams Auto. Somebody there tells me they can fix the flat, but he is very apologetic. "It might be a while before I can get to it," he says.

When I hear the phrase "a while," my heart sinks. Worst-case scenarios pop into my head. Tomorrow? Next week? Next month?

"It will be at least 11:00 a.m. before I can get to it," he tells me, still in an apologetic voice.

I breathe a sigh of relief at the estimate, which is far less than any of the worst-case scenarios that had popped to mind! At 11:00 a.m. on the nose, a mechanic grabs my keys. In twenty minutes he is back. The flat is fixed. It proved to be a small and easy leak, and it costs me a mere $25. I find an expensive market and buy a few supplies: veggies for dinner, a lighter for our campfire since we'd used the last of the matches, root beer for Yuki, an avocado for Julia, and some fresh banana bread as a treat for us all.

I stop at the Big Piney ranger station and get a map so that I can return to the Scaler cabin by a different route over a winding mountain. The folks there also give me a different number to reach Matt Anderson, the USFS fish and wildlife biologist in charge of the restoration program on La Barge whom I'd been trying unsuccessfully to reach for an interview for a couple weeks. As I drive away from civilization, back toward the national forest on a gravel road, I try repeatedly to reach Anderson before cell service disappears. My cell signal drops from four bars to three, and then from three to two, and then flickers to one. Just as my hopes fade with the bars, Anderson picks up. I pull the car over and we have a long conversation on the phone.

Matt Anderson seems quite happy to share his knowledge and insights with me. Although he will soon be leaving the Bridger Teton National Forest to work in different national forest, he has plenty of knowledge about the project. I get several bullet points' worth of important notes, ideas for more research, and also an important tidbit that will later bear fruit. The Colorado River cutthroat restoration project on La Barge Creek is a joint effort with Wyoming Game and Fish. He mentions Wyoming Game and Fish biologist Hilda Sexauer as one of the principles of the project. The work has also benefited from researchers at the University of Wyoming, including a current graduate student named Alex who is out at the project that day not far from our cabin—and whom I can probably find if I get back to the river before too late. (I will later learn that Trout Unlimited has also supported the project.) I learn that the fish passage barrier to prevent invasive rainbows from getting into the portions of La Barge Creek and its tributaries in the national forest was built between 2000 and 2002, and that the project had involved a couple rotenone treatments after the dam was built. When I later find Alex and his partner back on the river collecting data, I will learn from him that the project, in addition to the rotenone, also involved electro-shocking to remove invasive fish.

Our conversation turns from the removal of invasive fish to the restoration of habitat, and eventually to the issues that might be hindering the recovery of the native cutthroat. Matt describes five completed culvert removals or replacements to improve fish passage to upstream spawning habitats. A couple of culverts on the main stem were replaced with bridges using either concrete rectangular culverts or entirely natural bottoms. The culvert over the South La Barge just above the confluence was replaced with a bottomless culvert. (I get the locations of all of them and make a note to myself that we need to photograph or film then.) He also mentions a couple of projects on schedule for that year, and several more for the years to come. Having written about similar culvert replacement projects to restore native brook trout waters in Maine, I'm familiar with the costs. Matt confirms the ballpark figure of $20,000 per bridge is about right for the Wyoming work also.

Anderson then mentions that they are collecting meta-population data to see how successful the project has been. They have implanted some fish with passive integrative transmitters: P.I.T. tags for short. The solar arrays I have noticed in several places along the river power receivers that collect data from passing fish with these tags. And there is data! Some fish are surviving; they are moving around the river, swimming past the sensors with their P.I.T. tags. But the survival and reproduction numbers are lower than hoped for. Low enough—as I tell Matt Anderson—that my efforts to entice a fish with a fly or even to spot one, have so far all failed. But I also assure him from my unscientific observations that abundant insect life thrives in the rivers. Though more work remains to be done on the culverts, food and quality habitat shouldn't be the limiting factor.

So what is?

"The gene pool," Anderson conjectures. He is quick to acknowledge that it is only a conjecture, and they are testing it. Another conjecture is that the culverts they haven't yet replaced are actually the important ones in terms of passage to spawning habitat. But Anderson thinks the more likely issue is the strain of Colorado River cutthroat trout they have been using to restock La Barge. The wild fish they had used to restock La Barge had actually come from a lake-dwelling population, because that was the best source they had. Though still the same species (O.clarki) and even the same subspecies (O. c. pleuriticus), it was a strain of Colorado River cutthroat genetically adapted to an adfluvial life history, not a fluvial one; which is to say, the gene pool they had transplanted into the river to restore a native fish species was better suited for adult life in a lake, not a small mountain stream. If they could transplant a truly fluvial strain of Colorado River cutthroat from some nearby mountain stream, the chances of successful survival, reproduction, and ultimate repopulation would be much better, he thought.

A couple hours after saying goodbye to Anderson, following a beautiful drive along a winding forest service road near the east and south slopes of Wyoming Peak and Mount Darby, I approach the bridge over the South Fork of La Barge and the road back to our primitive cabin. There, as Anderson thought, I see a pickup truck by the roadside. The truck prominently displays a University of Wyoming sticker. It's only the third or fourth car I've seen in three days. I'm convinced it will be Alex before I even see him. I pull over and introduce myself, and I'm soon proved correct. Alex comes up to the cabin and we have an enjoyable conversation along with Yuki, Julia, and Andrew. He fills in a bit more detail beyond what I'd learned from Matt. His summary is that the project has shown some signs of success. But he agrees with Anderson on the need for a strain of the native Colorado River subspecies of cutthroat more closely adapted to the conditions of river life. They are now looking for some other sources they can use for transplant to the La Barge Creek and the Bridger-Teton National Forest. Nobody can really predict what will happen though. Not for the last time, I see how much more difficult it is to heal than it is to harm.

We say goodbye, and I wish Alex well. I'm still wishing him well, and all who are doing the important work of restoration.

We leave the Scalar Guard Station cabin mid-morning the next day and head northwest up the forest road. We are once again following the route of the Oregon Trail as we proceed upriver along La Barge Creek, crossing back and forth over it several times as we go, until it is just a small headwater stream that flows through a wide beaver meadow thick with brush. Wildflowers cover the open hills where small family groups of antelope roam. The antelope move further from the roads when our car stops and the humans emerge to take pictures of them. Some pause atop a distant slope letting us admire their silhouettes. Others disappear down the back side. We also pause to take photos of bridge crossings, including some that been replaced and now have natural stream bottoms friendly to fish migration.

At a junction, we turn north and soon cross over the Tri-Basin Divide, moving from the Colorado River watershed to that of the Columbia River—where the prevailing wisdom tells us that nearly all of the existing strains of cutthroat trout originated as they colonized their way upriver, crossed watersheds, become isolated, and over thousands of years continued to adapt to different local conditions. We soon come to the headwaters of Greys River and we follow its flow down into its own river valley. We stop for a picnic lunch while the valley is still narrow, and the river cascades and tumbles from pool to pool like a mountain brook. While picnicking, I spot a trout feeding in a small pool beside a large boulder. A promising sign! It is the first fish I've seen since leaving the impassable barrier on La Barge.

We continue down Greys River. The valley walls enclosing us grow farther apart. We watch the river grow as it snakes through progressively wider meadows. I look down from partway up the hillside where the road leads us and I see pools and bends I am sure hold trout. Unfortunately, it would take me an hour to scramble, wade, and bushwhack into them. And I have two other people with me.

So I keep on driving, further down into the wider valley. In the middle of a two-mile long stretch of mostly straight gravel road through a treeless stretch of terrain patched with dirt and green and brown grass, we find the Cazier Guard Station USFS cabin. The cabin will be our abode for the next two nights until we have to leave this national forest. The cabin sits beneath the hot midday Wyoming sun on flat river bottom land. In the background I can see a line of wooden fences from a corral of some sort. An outbuilding sports a solar panel on the roof. I use the combination supplied by the USFS to open the padlocked door and we step out of the hot sun into a hot cabin.

Compared with Scalar, Cazier is downright luxurious. Though it offers only a single large bunk room instead of three separate sleeping rooms, it has a working gas refrigerator and stove, solar-powered electric lights, and—best of all—indoor plumbing including a hot shower. We carry our belongings inside, claim bunks, and within thirty minutes Yuki and Julia are sound asleep, conquered by the irresistible call of an afternoon nap. I close my eyes and rest for a short while. But the cabin is hot, and the river is calling my name with an even more irresistible call. I've been in Wyoming for several days, in national forests surrounded by beautiful trout habitat, yet I still haven't held a fish in my hand. Later in the evening, when the lighting is softer, we will head out together to do some filming. Now I leave my students asleep and I step out quietly, pull on my waders, rig my fly rod, and start walking toward Greys River which runs along the edge of a bluff five hundred feet west of the cabin on the opposite side of the valley from the road.

Almost at once I drop down a steep bank, leaving the dry sparse grass for a jaunt across wet brushy terrain. Although I'm sweltering in my waders in the afternoon heat, when my feet find water, I'm glad I have wading boots on. Several wood fences suggest some sort of corral, but without a bird's eye view I don't have a good sense of its layout. One of the little side streams cutting through the brush follows a straight line and I guess it's a channel cut to provide water for animals that might be corralled there. My thoughts are too occupied with the river, however, to give it much thought. A minute later I'm at the edge of the river. As I look for a place to get through the riverside brush to the water, I spot a promising fishing spot almost immediately. An old man-made structure—perhaps a small diversion dam to send water out into the water troughs—angles across the stream, creating a plunge about a foot high. Below the drop, the river deepens as it swirls around both sides of a big boulder and then tails out where a small tributary tumbles in through some bushes on the other side.

I see several places a trout might hold in the pool, depending on how it's feeding. I make casts to the soft water at the edge of the seam where the current parts around the rock. Nothing hits. I work down the near shore swinging my fly through the tail-out. Nothing there either. I move back to the head of the pool and wade out a couple steps. The main channel runs against the far shore. I cast into the swift water underneath the stream-side bushes. A sudden tug pulses at the end of my line. Three or four seconds of excitement—just enough to catch sight of a flash of silver and red about ten inches long. Then the line stops pulsing.

I fish the pool another fifteen minutes working the riffs, the seams, the deep hole, the confluence. Nothing appears. I wade to the far shore, leave the pool behind me, and begin to work my way downriver. I cover a third of a mile, alternately wading and scrambling along a steep gravel bank, fishing my way down quickly because I don't see a lot of good trout habitat. As far as I go, the river is one long steady riffle, wide and shallow. It offers breeding habitat for insects, but no obvious holding water for a trout.

My hope of discovering a great stretch of fishing close to the cabin fades the farther I amble down the river. Finally, several bends downstream, I give up looking. To get a better view of the river and surrounding landscape, and because I'm tired of navigating a brushy shore, I scramble up a steep sandy bank at my back. From atop a bluff a dozen feet above the river, I gaze out over the valley. The added height provides good views for hundreds of yards in both directions. With the exception of one gap back where I'd first come to the river, the bluff on which I'm standing runs north and south along the west bank of Greys River as far as I can see.

I think again of the wagon trains on the Oregon Trail passing by more than a century and a half earlier on their life-changing adventure, just a little further along from La Barge Creek. Here I am, also just a little farther on from La Barge. Instead of a Conestoga Wagons stuffed with all I own and all my hopes for the future, I have a rented SUV packed with a month of clothing and camping gear, and a one-week supply of food. My own adventure will not be nearly as dangerous or as dramatic, though experiences such as this do have a way of shaping somebody. At present, my primary hope for the future is for the very near future: a hope that the near future will hold a cutthroat trout for me. Or that I will hold a cutthroat for my future.

I'm almost ready to give up finding one, however. I've been fishing Greys for an hour and a half without success. Not even a hint of success since that one strike in the first place I cast. I look downstream one more time. On the far side of the river, between the river and the road, the land looks marshy and thick with brush and young trees—verdant, full of life, but a very unpleasant place to have to traverse. From this higher vantage, however, I spot a pond a few dozen yards back from the river. Perhaps a cold tributary creek or braid of the main channel flows invisible under the thick foliage and feeds it a supply of cold well-aerated water. Perhaps it is deeper than it looks. Perhaps it holds trout.

More likely, it doesn't. In the hot Wyoming sun, a shallow pond with a black bottom heats quickly. I didn't fancy bushwhacking through the brush on a wild goose chase. I stay atop the bluff and walk the few hundred yards back upriver to where I started. In addition to the cooler breeze, and the break from bushwhacking, I also appreciate the view. I get a better sense of the layout of the area, including not only the path of the river but also the connected geometry of the various lines of fences. They definitely form a large enclosure. I wonder how old the corral is and whether it is still in use. The fence appears to be in good shape. I think of the 13,000 travelers passing over the Tri-Basin Divide in the summer of 1859 at the peak of the Oregon Trail travel. Though some of those parties turned left and followed the Bear River down into the Great Basin of what is now Utah, most turned right and began following this river downstream. Since those travelers had nearly 80,000 head of livestock, some sort of corral almost certainly dates all the way back to those days. All that livestock had to be kept somewhere. Somebody also took the time to cut that channel through the corral from the main river. Even today cattle ranchers graze livestock in parts of the national forest—a fact we experienced firsthand back at the Scalar Guard Service cabin—while other visitors bring horses up for recreational riding. Nonetheless, though the area around the cabin is kept clear, the corral looks overgrown and marshy.

I am almost back to where I started, at the top of the little bluff across the river from the cabin and from where I first cast my flies and saw the one fish. I look again at the small tributary flowing in from my right, cutting through the bluff I stand on. The map identifies it as Corral Creek. I make a connection between the creek name and the old fences. I get another hint that the Corral has been there a long time—since before that creek had a name. I had ignored Corral Creek when I waded past it earlier, and I'm tempted to do so again. It isn't more than four feet wide. What would bring a trout up there, that it couldn't find in the main river? From the bluff I can see a hundred yards upstream, and it looks even less promising than down near the confluence. Corral Creek tumbles fast and white down a steep gradient through overhanging bushes that would have made fishing next to impossible even if I had thought fish might be hanging out in that foamy water. But I wasn't ready to give up. I could see a bend upstream, as there always is. Just one more bend. And that next bend might be the one. It could be. It might be. I always think it might be. And sometimes, every once in a while, it actually is.

Trout or no trout, with the cool breeze and lovely views the walk up the smaller stream looks pleasant enough, and far more enjoyable than bushwhacking to the pond I'd seen. I descend to the shore and start up Corral Creek. For the first hundred yards I don't bother fishing. Two bends up, however, I come upon an old footbridge. It seems to lead from nowhere to nowhere. It does, however, provide a nice place to stand and look, as well as a safe and easy way across the creek.

And to get across is suddenly exactly what I want to do, because as I approach the bridge I see the creek bend around a tight oxbow, and on the far side—the upstream side—I catch a glimpse of an amazing-looking hole. Despite the clarity of the water, the pool is dark and deep, with a gorgeous riff on the upriver side, deep undercut banks around the back side, and a perfect tail-out that narrows into another riff and then a smaller but still enticing hole.

My heart beats with excitement at the best-looking piece of water I've seen since walking out the cabin. I approached carefully, formulating a plan for how to entice any residents with an artificial fly. It looks as perfect from up close as it did from back on the bridge. I can't see the bottom. It might be over my head. It's a very deep pool for a river this small. A veritable mansion for a community of trout, ruled over by some wise old dictator. The swirls and eddies will make it difficult to get a dry fly to drift properly unless I wade through the brush and approach from below, working around the oxbow. I decide on a different strategy. Hoping to get a fly down deep to a big lunker, I tie on a streamer: an imitation of a little forage fish. Approaching the bank cautiously on the upstream side of the hole, I take a sequence of casts with twitching strips, each one getting a little farther out into the pool.

On the fifth or sixth cast a monster trout rises from the depths of the pool and slams my fly just below the surface. With one vigorous shake of its head, it snaps my line. Brand new 5x tapered leader I had just put on that day should have had a breaking strength of four pounds. My heart thumps harder thinking about that.

I tie on another fly and take several more casts, working more of the pool, but I don't see another fish. In hopes that the lunker might get unspooked, I decide to leave the hole and head upstream for a while. I navigate around more bushes trying to spot more promising water. I don't have to go far. Within sight of the first hole, I spot another beautiful bend in the creek. This one is not as deep, but it's longer with another undercut bank on the outside of the bend. It also has soft water both on the inside of the bend and behind some jutting banks on the outside. Unlike the lower hole, it ends by spreading out into a wide shallower pool instead of narrowing into another run. Only when I stand down at the stream edge do I see the low beaver dam that forms the pool. I see no sign of a beaver or a beaver house.

To avoid casting in the bushes, I wade across to approach the hole from upstream. There I swing a streamer against the far bank, the outer side of the bend. About halfway around I started getting swirls and misses at my fly. Then I get a hard hit. Another streamer breaks off.

I tie on a new fly and this time I test the leader more aggressively. The new tippet breaks off in my hand more easily than it should. I make a note not to buy that brand anymore. Impatient though I am to fish, I take the extra time to change out my entire 5x tapered leader and put on some 4x. Five minutes later I land a fat cutthroat trout from beneath the far bank of the upper pool. Keeping it wet in the net underwater, I look it over carefully and take a few photos. It is a Snake River Fine-Spotted, a strain—or some say a subspecies—of the more famous Yellowstone Cutthroat. It is native to this water, a tributary of the Snake River.

Plans for the next two days form. I need to bring Julia back here so she can catch one. And I need to bring Yuki here to do some videoing. We might get the underwater footage we have been looking for. And, of course, I need to return to the deeper lower hole and try for that lunker again.

I think also of what I learned and experienced over the previous three days of exploration just a few dozen miles south of here on a different watershed where a different strain of cutthroat trout once thrived. The thought makes me especially delighted to find this fish.

I do return a couple more times over the next two days. I bring Julia and Yuki here in the evening light. We catch more fish. Yuki gets some good footage for our project. Julia holds a wild native trout. We explore farther up the stream, too, and find several more trout. In fact, I find some in almost every stretch of good looking water I take the time to cast a fly into.

And on the last evening I return again, alone. I try once more for the big lunker, but it never shows up. But I do succeed in catching two fish in the very first hole I tried, fishing probably a little too late into the darkness before feeling my way across the river and back to the cabin for my last night before heading off to the Shoshone National Forest and Yellowstone National Park. I leave with memories of some fine-spotted trout on Corral Creek. Perhaps not as dramatically as it did for the Oregon Trail travelers, the place has nonetheless changed me.

Grizzly at Pelican Creek

Yellowstone National Park and the Shoshone National Forest Popo Agie Wilderness

"Lake trout kill elk," he told me. It was a bumper sticker motto. But it was also a serious statement, and I understood why.

I had just spent ten days traveling and researching native cutthroat trout in two national forests and one national park in western Wyoming. Middlebury College students Julia and Yuki joined me as research and video assistants. We saw numerous cutthroat trout. A few had danced at the end of my fly line, but many we simply observed—and filmed, from both above and below the water surface—feeding, swimming, hiding, and living in their native environments in various rivers and streams we had visited. We'd also seen one small herd of elk: five cows and three calves in a quiet shaded meadow just two hundred yards down the road from a Yellowstone traffic jam where dozens of cars paused to watch a single large bull nap in the sunshine on a less-scenic front lawn of a park building.

Best of all, we also enjoyed watching three grizzly bears. The timing of seeing a sow and cub was perfect. We were climbing over Sylvan Pass on the way from Yellowstone National Park to the Shoshone National Forest. Julia and Yuki asked if we could see some grizzlies. I promised I'd do my best. And a few corners later we approached another traffic jam, this one at 8,500 feet in elevation. Yellowstone traffic jams nearly always mean wildlife, and it took only a few seconds to spot the objects of attention. We pulled into the line of parked cars, took out our cameras, and (from a safe distance) watched for several minutes as a sow-cub pair of bruins browsed along a hillside just above the road. The hefty cub even pandered to the cameras for a moment, climbing up on a fallen log and playing clumsy gymnast.

The other bear-sighting was two days later on an early morning wildlife drive, returning over the same pass back into the park. We spotted the big brown bear swimming across a cove of Yellowstone Lake. I pulled our car over, this time without any traffic jam, and watched as it stepped into the shallows, shook itself off like a big wet dog, and wandered up onto shore, across the road, and off over a meadow. In those three bears, especially the final one, was the connection between the lake trout, the cutthroat trout, and the elk—or, rather, one of many links in an intricate web of interconnectedness we were just beginning to understand.

The central part of that earlier travel, though, was the time spent on La Barge Creek in the Bridger-Teton National Forest, learning about and observing firsthand the ongoing efforts to restore native Colorado River cutthroat. The area had a long history of habitat degradation—over-grazing, deforestation, mining, river-unfriendly road and bridge building, water diversion—dating back at least to the days of the Oregon Trail. Yet despite all of the ecological damage to river ecology, most biologists agree that the deadliest blow to cutthroat populations throughout the Rockies has been caused by the introduction of non-native trout species, a practice already widespread by the end of the 19th century. These exotic trout destroyed populations of the native cutthroat through predation and competition, and (in the case of invasive rainbow trout) through hybridization, in some places causing the complete extinction of entire subspecies.

The La Barge Creek project had already been going on for fifteen years when we visited. I know that some people question whether such efforts and expenses—the removal of invasive fish, creation of artificial barriers, transplanting wild cutthroat from another location, and the ongoing work of habitat restoration—are really worthwhile. Why does it matter whether cutthroat trout remain in their native lakes and streams? Why not just accept the invasive rainbow, brook, and lake trout? I'd heard these questions more than once.

As we sat by the La Barge Creek or explored the quiet and secluded valley, it was hard to imagine the area bustling and degraded by crowds of settlers or noisy lumber camps. We saw moose, mule deer, and pronghorn antelopes wander the meadows and forested hillsides while bald eagles flew overhead and songbirds serenaded us from the woods. Beaver activity was present all up and down the valley. The river itself was bursting with life, especially aquatic invertebrates. In the late morning, clouds of mayflies rose in columns behind the cabin, twenty, thirty, forty yards into the air above the river in such numbers they were visible on video against the dark hillside. The afternoon saw hatches of caddis flies that swarmed the riparian bushes from which they bounced like yoyos down to the stream surface to lay eggs and then back up to the bushes. In the evening, tiny midges looked like a layer of fog laying a foot above the water. And all day long, in ones and twos, small green and grey stoneflies drifted past us.

What we didn't see on the river, however, were cutthroat trout. There was work yet to be done before the project could be deemed a success. So we moved on to other rivers where native cutthroat once swam, slowly making our way north. Leaving La Barge Creek, where Colorado River cutthroat were native, we turned north. We spent a couple days on

Greys River, also in the Bridger-Teton National Forest, where we were delighted to find an abundant population of the native Snake River Fine-Spotted cutthroat. From there we traveled to numerous waters in the Shoshone National Forest, finding both abundant non-native trout and also some wild cutthroat. We also took two excursions to visit the famous Yellowstone River and Yellowstone Lake where native Yellowstone cutthroat still swam. These trips, though brief, may have been the most informative in terms of answering the questions.

Yellowstone Lake once held the largest population of cutthroat trout in the world. Hundreds of thousands of them spawned both downriver and up the lake's major tributaries, including Pelican Creek near where we had seen the third grizzly bear. When such large numbers of cutthroat move into the rivers and streams to spawn, they represent a tremendous amount of available nutrition to all manner of predators. Osprey are specialized fish eaters, largely dependent on cutthroat for their diet. Bald eagles also prey on them, as do mink and otters. There is even a population of American white pelicans living by this high-elevation inland lake. The creek is not gratuitously named. Pelicans live there because the native cutthroat trout provide a wonderful and important food source. And the cutthroat-borne nutrition goes beyond the fauna to the flora because all those cutthroat-eating birds and mammals spread the nutrition out into the soil surrounding the rivers, enabling all sorts of plants to thrive and provide habitat and food for other creatures that don't feed directly on the native trout.

Then there are the Yellowstone grizzlies. They feed on the spawning cutthroat the way Alaskan brown bears feed on salmon. A few decades ago, however, invasive lake trout somehow found their way into the lake, presumably through illegal human stocking. The lake trout, like most large salmonids, are piscivores. Indeed, they are voracious predators. They gorge on cutthroat, especially the young ones moving down to the lake from the spawning redds where they hatched from eggs. Thus after the introduction of lake trout into the Yellowstone Lake, the population of Yellowstone cutthroat trout began to crash. Suddenly the most important food supply for so many other creatures disappeared. Lake trout, though abundant and large and full of protein, are not available to other creatures. Unlike the cutthroat trout they were supplanting, lake trout don't spawn in shallow streams and rivers; they spawn in the lake and spend most of the year in deep water. They are not food for eagles or mink or pelicans or bears. Or for osprey, a beautiful and athletic species of eagle that feeds almost exclusively on fish, and is known for breathtaking dives straight into the water from hundreds of feet in the air. In the 1970s, there were between sixty and sixty-five active pairs of osprey around the lake, well-fed by the healthy population of cutthroat. By 2013, a few decades after the illegal introduction of lake trout, there were only five remaining pairs, and only two produced offspring.

The cutthroat had coevolved with the entire ecosystem. Just as they were adapted to that water, so the creatures around them were adapted to the cutthroat and their life cycles. There were mutual interdependencies everywhere. Anglers may enjoy catching non-native rainbow trout—or lake trout, or brook trout—in famous western rivers and lakes, but one species of trout is not the same as another. The exotic game species are not the same as the native fish. It does indeed matter that the rivers hold native fish. It may matter a great deal.

This brings me back to the grizzly bears. When the cutthroat trout population crashed because of the invasive lake trout, the bears—now deprived of this supply of protein once abundantly available to them during the spawning season in late spring or early summer—had to go elsewhere for their diet. They began to prey more heavily on young elk. Thus with the decline of cutthroat trout, the elk population began to decline also. Hence the slogan on the bumper sticker. Lake trout really do kill elk, though in a rather roundabout way.

Fortunately for the Yellowstone Lake cutthroat trout, and equally fortunately for the creatures co-adapted for thousands of years to feed upon them—and for a whole eco-system heavily dependent upon these native fish—since the original crash of the Yellowstone cutthroat populations, federal as well as private groups like Trout Unlimited have worked in collaboration to reduce and control the lake trout population. It is an expensive, ongoing task, one that will likely have to continue in perpetuity. But over the past two or three years it has shown signs of success. Cutthroat populations are rebounding.

Sitting in a National Forest Service office in Cody with the fisheries biologist working in the Shoshone National Forest, we watched a video recently taken from a trail camera on a cutthroat spawning stream. The video showed a grizzly bear catching and eating a spawning cutthroat. I imagined that scene once again playing out not only in the Shoshone National Forest where the video was taken, but also in the numerous tributaries to Yellowstone Lake, and maybe someday in La Barge Creek.

A week after our visit to Yellowstone, Julia and Yuki and I, along with my friend Phil and his son Rob, took a week-long trip to the Popo Agie Wilderness Area in Wyoming's Wind River Mountains. For five nights, we camped at 10,000 feet beside a small river where brook trout—another human-introduced exotic invader of the Rocky Mountains—competed with cutthroat trout for food. We sat for hours beside a small waterfall in the middle of the woods watching (and filming) both cutthroat and brook trout attempting to leap upstream to colonize new waters. During peak activity in the middle of the afternoon, we saw as many as four fish per minute jumping. Some made it. Most fell back. I imagined how the cutthroat colonized the Rockies over tens and hundreds of thousands of years, working their way up small tributary streams and eventually finding their way through high-elevation ponds up and over divides and into new watersheds. Over long geologic periods of time they adapted to isolated local environments, and other creatures adapted to them. I also saw how quickly and determinedly invasive species like brook trout could colonize new water once introduced.

At the end of our trip, enjoying a wonderful meal back at the Allens Diamond 4 Ranch after a long horseback ride back out of the mountains, we commented to our host and the wrangler who had led the trip about how much we had enjoyed our time. We described the many large cutthroat trout we had seen in the river. Another of the guests, preparing to depart on his own fishing trip, made a dismissive comment about the cutthroat, saying how much he preferred catching rainbow trout. I had to bite back my response and refrain from giving a long professorial lecture that would probably have fallen on deaf ears. "Yeah", I wanted to say about his preferred fish. "But did you know they kill elk?"

II.
Westslope Cutthroat
(and an Artist Residency)

Stories from Glacier National Park
and Flathead National Forest

In April of 2017, I received a call that I had been selected as a 2020 Artist-in-Residence at Glacier National Park.
I was invited to spend the month of June residing in an art-
ists' cabin on the upper (northeast) end of Lake McDonald,
visiting the park as an official NPS volunteer. No internet.
No phone service. Just a month to learn about the park and
to tell stories through narrative non-fiction writing as well
as photographs and videos and digital story-telling forms.[23]

My application explicitly listed as foci of my narratives
both river ecology and native fish: Westslope cutthroat trout
and bull trout. The latter of these, despite a common name
associating them with Salmo trutta (European brown trout)
are a species of char *(Salvelinus confluentus)* more closely related to Arctic char *(S. alpinus)*, brook trout *(S. fontinalis)*
and lake trout *(S. namaycush)* than to cutthroat. Except, unlike brook trout and lake trout, bull trout are native to the
west slope of the Rockies and for millennia have co-adapted
to live in the same waters as cutthroat trout. As with many
subspecies of cutthroat trout further south, the populations
of both these native species in the northern Rockies—

23   Video essays from this experience may be viewed on the YouTube
Trout Downstream and Heart Streams channel on the "Glacier National
Park and Flathead National Forest" playlist: www.youtube.com/playlist?
list=PLmBeEX5ze8pr3rV8PEu9Hz2IQrw_bSz2K.

including within Glacier National Park—have been dramatically and negatively impacted by the presence of invasive fish. Bull trout have been listed as an endangered species since 1980, and their plight has not improved since then.

One of my earlier books, *The Voices of Rivers* (2019), shares in narrative non-fiction form many of my stories and essays from this time, conveying much of what I learned about the ecology and history, the landscapes and breathtaking beauty, and both the resiliency and fragility of Glacier National Park. One of the great opportunities that came out of the residency was spending time with knowledgeable biologists from both the National Park Service and the U.S.G.S. who worked in and around the park, especially Christopher Downs and Clint Muhlfeld (whom I mentioned and acknowledged in the introduction to this book). In fact, my experience within the park and adjacent national forest was so informative that it could have supplied narrative material for many books. I left out of my earlier book many stories, especially those most focused on cutthroat trout and on fly fishing. My goal was to include them here instead, in a collection with a narrower topic (native cutthroat trout), but a broader geographic range (national parks and national forests across Wyoming and Montana, and not just the greater Glacier National Park area.)

Of Beaver Dams and Mosquitos

Morning. June 8, 2017

It's the fourth day of my artist residency at Glacier National Park. I wake an hour later than I did yesterday. Although still early, it's also an hour later than I planned to rise, and not quite early enough to get somewhere for the 5:30 a.m. sunrise. I blame my tardy start on the previous evening's excursion with two park employees to a small lake whose beaver-dam outlet poured into a series of three pools packed full of native Westslope cutthroat trout. The males were displaying their extravagant spawning colors: mottled red underbellies, almost purple pelvic fins, and red gill covers reminiscent of their steelhead cousins, all contrasting with the softer yellow green sides, green tails, and their famous ruby necklaces that have earned their species its common name. I was also becoming more aware of how the patterns of black spots varied from one cutthroat subspecies to another. The spots of the Westslope Cutthroat are definitely larger than those on the Snake River Fine-Spotted cutthroat, and run from tail to head, though they are more densely packed closer to the tail, on the dorsal fins, and above the lateral line. On the front half of the body below the lateral line, they are quite sparse. Do the differing spot patterns reflect some sort of survival advantage in different types of water—perhaps a better or worse camouflage against a stream bottom?

In the back of my mind I'm also still pondering the question of what those trout were doing below the beaver dam. Had they been attempting to migrate upstream into the lake, but found their passage blocked by the beaver dam? Or were they perhaps lake residents: adfluvial outlet-spawning fish who had dropped down over the dam to the stream below in obedience to their reproductive drive?

Mostly, though, my mind still basks in the delighted afterglow of the whole experience, first watching and videoing, and then casting flies into, that pool full of beautiful, brightly colored trout. I enticed a few of them to my net for additional photos before releasing them back to join their friends. I've fished many fantastic tail-water fisheries below manmade dams, and caught much larger trout in a few of them, but I've rarely had a more enjoyable hour than I had the previous evening at that beaver-dam tail-water. And it wasn't just the fish that brought so much delight. When we arrived, the lake provided one of those mirrored reflections of the park's famous peaks—in June still capped with a significant amount of snow—that make it difficult to stop taking pictures even when all the photos are clichéd and nearly identical. To top it all off, just before we left, as dusk was settling in, a pair of beavers came out to entertain us, which one of them did by repeatedly swimming past us and slapping its tail on the water and diving. The entertainment, followed by the slow drive back to my cabin, kept me up later than planned, resulting in the later morning. Or maybe I was only getting better adjusted from East Coast time to Rocky Mountain Time.

Still pondering the evening, I eat breakfast, make a thermos of coffee, and head out on a not-quite-as-early-as-hoped morning drive past the head of Lake McDonald. Between the Lake and Avalanche Creek, I pull over at a trail head and park my car near a foot bridge that crosses McDonald Creek. I enjoy the thunder of the river below me and take video footage of it from the bridge. Then I head up a trail on the far side of the river. Upper McDonald Creek looks like a different river today as I walk alongside it—and not just because I'm an hour later, on the opposite shore, and underneath a blanket of low gray clouds. Though all of those changes are noticeable, the real difference is the river level. This morning my thermometer reads 60°. It did not cool off nearly as much last night as the night before, and so the snow continued to melt through the night at a much higher rate. Today the river rages. Glacial silt fills the water, turning it a cloudy whitish green. Visibility has dropped from a few feet to a few inches. Water rips through areas where the day before I had spotted slack water. This stretch of river is known for particularly poor fishing, but even were that not the case I would have no temptation to return to the cabin and get my fly rod. Not in the main channel, anyway. I'm hoping to discover something up that little side channel, though. The previous evening's experience has my imagination fixed on beaver dams—and on the possibility of trout above or below them. So I follow the path several hundred yards up the shoreline looking for a tributary I thought I had spotted from the road on the other side.

Sure enough, I come to the place I had seen. The channel flowing in from the side is too wide and deep to cross. The trail turns left along the inlet and I follow it another fifty or sixty yards into the woods, away from Upper McDonald Creek. And there I find the beaver's dam I'd been hoping for: a long one that bends around to the right spanning a couple hundred feet from the near shore to the bushes where I can no longer see it. The water above and below is much clearer than the raging silt-filled current of the river. There are no rapids here, and no sign of melting glacier or snowpack. It looks like a great home for waterfowl. Or a moose.

I wander up and down for a few moments, taking more photos and scouting for signs of trout in the clear water. I see no trout. I see no beaver. Unlike around the Avalanche Creek parking area, I also so no other humans. I do see ducks, though none close enough to identify. I see a few mosquitoes too. More importantly, the mosquitos see me. I put on gloves, and cover my head and arms. Then I unpack my chair and sit down to listen, think, and write.

Have I mentioned that I love beavers? I love beavers themselves almost as much as I love discovering one of their ponds on some out-of-the-way trout stream in the mountains. I love watching them swim and work. When I think of otters, I think of play. When I think of beavers, I think of work. Yet maybe that distinction is irrelevant with animals; maybe their work is play and vice versa. I love how much beavers can accomplish. A mature beaver's dam like this one is a thing to behold: a marvel of engineering. I love how this wild, native, natural animal—smaller than all of the dogs I've ever owned—can so dramatically shape the ecology of a whole valley.

Long before this beaver pond silts over and becomes a beaver meadow, the beavers here—descendants of the original builders perhaps—will abandon the dam and move on up the valley, or down, or across the ridge to the next valley to colonize a new stream. Decades from now the forest will begin to colonize the meadow, just as it has been colonizing the mountain slopes and the valleys from which glaciers have retreated. It is not unlike the way cutthroat trout pushed up the Columbia River in order to colonize the Rocky Mountains millennia ago, or the way both cutthroat and brook trout were attempting to climb the little waterfalls upstream of our campsite to colonize the South Fork of the Little Wind River.

I keep my camera at hand, in case the beaver appears. I keep bear spray at hand also. My gaze moves between the distant snowy peaks visible through gaps in the canopy, the reflection of those trees and mountains in yet another beaver-made mirror, and the water easing past below me where I keep hoping for a sign of a trout sipping food on the surface or moving around a fallen log.

Wind soughs through the trees. In the distance I hear the roar of the swollen river. Nearer at hand, the more gentle and steady gurgle of water spilling over the dam makes most of the sound track, though it is punctuated by the occasional warble or trill of a songbird. The sound of crunching in the brush makes me spin my head, but I never have cause to grab my bear spray. Neither does any beaver give me reason to grab the camera. Nor does a cutthroat appear and give me reason to return with a fly rod.

On the way back to the car, a tiny songbird alights on a branch a few feet in front of me. I don't see it at first. It sings a beautiful melody as I search eagerly for it. About the time I spot it on a branch only ten feet in front of my nose and lift my camera toward it, it flies off. I catch only a quick glimpse. I have no time to observe any characteristic feature that might help me identify it. It was not much bigger than a golf ball and as drab as the bark of the tree. I can't even remember its song, except that it was beautiful.

Sun peaks over the mountains and briefly penetrates the clouds as I walk back to the car. The sun offers only a false promise, however. The clouds look no less thick. Thunderstorms are in the forecast. I returned to my car and back to the cabin still thinking of beavers and cutthroat. I spend most of the rest of the day in my cabin writing. In the late afternoon I drive along the lake to Apgar to explore the area a little and make use of the public WIFI at the Visitor's Center. As I drive back along the lake at 6:00 p.m., the thunderstorm that had been predicted for 2:00 p.m. make its presence known with distance flashes and low rumbles. I make it into the cabin just in time. Thunder rolls. Lightning lights up the sky around me. Rains pound down, and heavy winds roil up the lake and send whitecaps breaking on the shore in front of my cabin. I'm glad I did my walking and outside writing in the morning.

Hungry Horse Reservoir
and Flathead National Forest

June 11 and July 21

It's Sunday morning at the end of my first week in Glacier National Park. After a quick breakfast, I head west out of the park for my first excursion to Columbia Falls for a mocha and pastry, followed by a worship service at a local church, then a trip to the grocery store to replenish my food supplies. After lunch, I head back east, up the Flathead River in the direction of the park entrance. When I cross the South Fork, however, rather than continuing on toward the park, I veer to the south onto a back road toward the vastness of Flathead National Forest. I'm hesitant to spend time outside of Glacier National Park because there is so much to see within the park. Indeed, there is far more to see than I have time for. I need a decade-long residency. Yet I want to make at least a couple visits to the adjacent national forest while I am in northern Montana so close to its boundaries.

The entire watershed of McDonald Creek sits inside of Glacier National Park: all the little feeder creeks that tumble off the ridges and mountain slopes into Upper McDonald Creek or directly into Lake McDonald, and then down the lower portion of the creek for its two-mile run to its confluence with the Middle Fork of the Flathead. The Middle Fork of the Flathead cascades northward out of the protection of the Great Bear Wilderness in the Flathead National Forest to the village of Nimrod, where the much smaller Bear Creek joins from the east. For the rest of its length, the Middle Fork runs along the boundary between the national park and the national forest, with the park to the northeast and the national forest to the southwest. All its tributaries flow in from one or the other of the two undeveloped areas. The North Fork of the Flathead which flows south out of Canada continues the boundary between the national park and national forest almost to its confluence with the Middle Fork four and a half miles downstream of the terminus of the McDonald Creek. None of these three rivers are dammed, and all of McDonald Creek and the Middle Fork along with the U.S. portions of the North Fork up to their confluence flow through public lands of the Flathead National Forest and the Glacier National Park.[24]

The South Fork of the Flathead River has a different story. Though it joins the combined waters of the Middle Fork and North Fork less than ten river miles downstream of their confluence, and though its headwaters also emerge from the public lands of the Flathead National Forest, the difference is a significant one: a large dam known as Hungry Horse. Hungry Horse Reservoir, squeezed between two rows of peaks with its dam at the north-northeast corner about five miles upriver from the main stem, impounds the waters of the South Fork. Thus its dam fractures the continuity of this otherwise contiguous and unfragmented river system. The reservoir is long and narrow—about thirty-five miles in length and 24,000 acres in area—surrounded by rugged parts of the Flathead National Forest. Much of its shoreline is inaccessible. The Hungry Horse Dam took five years to build

---

24 Along the North Fork and Middle Fork of the Flathead River, as well as adjacent to Lake McDonald on the McDonald Creek watershed, are small enclaves of grandfathered private land predating the national parks and national forests.

and was the second highest concrete dam in the world in 1953, the year it was finished and that it submerged one of the best stretches of whitewater in Montana in addition to a USFS fire tower.

Thinking and writing about the dam, I am reminded again of the environmental costs of river fragmentation. From a young age I understood and lamented the impact of dams on anadromous species like salmon. I have spent all but four years of my life living in Vermont, Massachusetts, New Hampshire, or Maine. What the first three of these have in common is the Connecticut River. And what all four of them once had in common were Atlantic salmon. Although loss of spawning habitat has certainly played a role in the demise of salmon in general, dams on the Connecticut River and the numerous rivers of Maine are the primary reason why Atlantic salmon are almost gone from New England. The main stem of the Connecticut alone has sixteen dams, the oldest dating back to the late eighteenth century. Counting all of its tributaries, there are more than a thousand dams throught the watershed. Millions of dollars spent over many years to bring Atlantic salmon back to the dammed (and doomed) Connecticut bore almost no fruit. When Tropical Storm Irene destroyed the salmon hatchery in Vermont's White River a decade ago, the federal government finally abandoned the attempt to restore anadromous salmon to that watershed. What little success Maine has had in restoring Atlantic salmon has come as a result of dam removal.

On the opposite side of the continent, Pacific salmon populations on the mighty Columbia River—three states and hundreds of miles downriver from the Flathead— have been similarly devastated by dams. The Columbia and its tributary the Snake River, even as they provided the routes for the colonization of North America by cutthroat trout over the past million years, also once served as a major spawning highway for anadromous salmon to reach all the way inland across Washington State and through landlocked Idaho. At one time, the Columbia produced the most commercial fish of any river in the United States. That was before the dams.

What I didn't understand until recently was how important long unfragmented stretches of river with a variety of habitats are, even to populations of non-anadromous freshwater fish. I grew up with the impression that a typical small-stream trout spends its entire life sitting in one pool, or one short stretch of larger river, except maybe during spawning season when it might swim a hundred yards upstream looking for a mate or a good spawning redd. This wasn't a result merely of my own ignorance. Until the mid 1980s, it was the prevailing scientific view, passed along as popular (though false) "wisdom". Kurt Fausch is one of the fisheries biologists whose work with trout and stream ecology has shown that view to be incorrect. What his research helped illuminate—and what my scientific reading has made clearer to me over the past decade—is that trout (and many other fish) over the entire course of their lifecycles need more than just one short piece of water with good habitat. Disconnected stream segments may support a small number of fish for a short time, but they don't support a healthy population. The situation is not unlike that of the monarch butterfly. An individual, or even an entire generation, may feed primarily on milkweed in a small section of Vermont. But the population as a whole needs the protected forests in a particular area of the mountains of Mexico, as well as food and habitat along the entire route between the two places. Fish also need different types of water at different times in the year or in their life histories. And for genetic diversity, different portions of a population also need to be connected to allow interaction of a broader gene pool.

In his book *For the Love of Rivers,* Fausch writes of this fragmenting impact on fish populations. "Even fish that do not migrate to an ocean can make important movements along streams, connecting one part of a watershed to another."[25] He points out how dams confine fish "to short stream segments, preventing their migrations and movements to find the habitats they need for spawning, rearing, and over-winter refuges."[26] His scientific research in Colorado and elsewhere made his conclusions clear:

> We now know that even some small fish only 3 inches long may need to traverse 50 miles or more of river, crossing many boundaries to find all the habitats they need to complete their life cycle. . . Without free access to deep, stable pools with abundant logs or undercut banks, and clean gravel riffles in which to lay their eggs, trout will either die during winter or be unable to spawn, and their numbers will decline. Anything we do as humans to disrupt these movements of invertebrates and fish across these boundaries will prove to reduce these animals that we may care about, as surely as we humans would also be reduced if our food and shelter were denied us.[27]

USGS fisheries biologist Clint Muhlfeld and National Parks fisheries biologist Christopher Downs, both of whom work in Glacier National Park, also spoke to me about the importance of having genetically diverse populations of the same species of fish—particularly the Westslope cutthroat

---

25 Fausch, *For the Love of Rivers,* 79.
26 Ibid., 25.
27 Ibid., 76.

trout native to the park—with different types of life histories. Within the subspecies are both fluvial populations with individuals spending their entire lives in rivers and streams, and adfluvial fish which spawn up rivers and streams but return as adult to live in bigger lakes. Even among the fluvial strains, some inhabit and are adapted to small alpine streams and others to larger rivers. Some may indeed spend much of their lives in a short stretch of river, but others travel great distances. A similar comment can be made about the native bull trout. They are known to travel a hundred miles or more to spawn. As with the stream-blocking culverts I wrote about earlier in this book, dams fragment rivers and prevent this important migration, potentially eliminating from the gene pool the trout with more complex life histories. Except that big concrete dams do this far more completely than a little culvert. Whereas some culverts, while significantly hindering migration, might allow an occasional fish to pass, a dam forms a complete blockade against any upriver movement.

Fragmenting of rivers is not the only negative environmental impact of dams. Dams also disturb both streamflow and water temperatures, and do so even more dramatically than the culverts I wrote about on La Barge Creek. The reservoirs formed by dams may also "drown" vital habitat such as spawning beds. Depending on the type of dam and the way it releases water, dams can either warm or cool the water coming out. Either of these results can be catastrophic to fish populations. Likewise, the scouring activity of a flood—which dams eliminate, intentionally or as a by-product—while often undesirable to humans, can be of great benefit to river ecology. Fausch is clear on this as well: "Controlling the natural flood disturbances with dams can cause a collapse of the food web."[28] Ironically, after hydroelectric generation, the second purpose of the Hungry Horse Dam is flood control. So flood control—despite its resulting negative impact on ecosystems—is not merely collateral, but intentional.

The road crosses the South Fork of the Flathead River below the Hungry Horse Dam and just above its confluence with the main stem of the Flathead. I had already crossed over the main stem of the Flathead coming out of Columbia Falls, and followed it for several miles along its south bank. Glancing down into the water I could see a silt-filled (and unfishable) turmoil. In my previous book, *The Voices of Rivers*, I described the June appearance of the Middle Fork two dozen miles upriver as looking like a kale smoothie with the blender still running. Where the bridge crosses the South Fork, however, the contrast is dramatic. Thanks in part to the dam and the impounded waters of Hungry Horse Reservoir, the waters flow much clearer. The South Fork looks very fishable—and indeed, as I learn from local guides, it gets fished much earlier in June than the other forks.

I also think of all the "great fishing" I've had in my life in the tail-waters below manmade dams on rivers like the Cumberland in Kentucky, the South Fork of the Holston in Tennessee, the San Juan in New Mexico, the Whitewater in Arkansas, the South Platte in Colorado, the Colorado River at Lee's Ferry in Arizona, and the Bighorn on the opposite corner of Montana from where I now am. By "great fishing", I mean that I have caught lots of big fish. But I have done so

<hr />

28 Fausch, *For the Love of Rivers*, 218.

in an unnatural environment, even when I was out of sight of the concrete edifice. And in every one of those tail-water examples, the fish I caught in large sizes and large numbers were non-native: most often rainbow trout or brown trout. Often, the native species fish can no longer survive downstream of the dam where the river habitat no longer resembles what they are adapted to. Much as I have enjoyed catching large tail-water trout, the knowledge of the environmental impact of the dams has made it more difficult to delight in those catches. As with so many other areas of life, my fishing adventures would be more blissful without this uncomfortable knowledge.

And yet—despite the harm they have caused to fish and river ecology through fragmentation and changes to river flows—in a few cases dams have proved to be a mixed blessing, environmentally speaking. On the South Fork of the Flathead, Hungry Horse Dam is an effective barrier to the upstream migration of invasive lake trout and rainbow trout from Flathead Lake, much like the artificial barrier constructed on La Barge Creek intentionally for that purpose. We often hear of collateral damage. This is a case of collateral (and unintended) benefit. Glacier National Park, while having the important feature of undammed rivers and an interconnected river ecosystem, has also had to deal with the devastating invasion of lake trout over the past three decades, as well as long term negative impact of rainbow trout on native cutthroat. Invasive lake trout moving up from Flathead Lake have resulted in the extirpation of bull trout from eight of the twelve lakes in the Flathead drainage where native populations of bull trout thrived only a few decades ago. And the native cutthroat trout in these rivers will be continually hybridized with the invasive rainbow trout until the original native strain of westslope cutthroat no longer exists in much of its native westslope range.

So despite the ecological harm it has caused—the fragmentation and the loss of miles of river habitat—the Hungry Horse Dam means that the watershed of the South Fork is free of invasive rainbow and lake trout. The cutthroat trout and bull trout populations in and above the reservoir remain intact.

It is a search for some of those native Westslope cutthroat that brings me down into the national forest for my first adventure there. While the Middle and North Forks remain unfishable from spring runoff, I have been told that some of the small tributaries flowing into the reservoir are good places to find wild native cutthroat trout in early June. My drive takes me down the eastern shore of the lake, and up one of those small tributaries: the reservoir's namesake creek. The dirt forest road crosses several smaller creeks—Margaret, Tiger, and Lost Mare Creeks—which flow from left to right under the road and down into Hungry Horse Creek. With the exception of a couple glimpses earlier on, Hungry Horse Creek remains out of sight somewhere off in the woods to my right—its presence known to me only from the map and the shape of the land. Were it a little Vermont trout stream in the familiar (to me) terrain of the Green Mountain National Forest, I might simply park the car and bushwhack down to it. I am, however, in a vast and unknown (to me) terrain, and moreover one inhabited by grizzly bears. The forest is thick with brush and fallen trees. Visibility in places does not go behind a few dozen feet. Also, nobody knows where I am. A decision to bushwhack off into the unknown, therefore, might be lacking in wisdom.

After following the creek four miles up to top of the hill without finding a good place to access it, I turn and come back down driving even more slowly. I pause by one of the feeder creeks, wondering if I might follow it downstream to Hungry Horse. Despite its small size, however, it tumbles down a steep gradient and at this time of year is still too swift and deep to wade, with thick brush on both banks. Finally I spot a bit of a clearing, with forty or fifty yards of visibility into the woods. I pull over the car and decide to explore. I walk to the end of the clearing, and there I find a relatively open path through the trees. Making plenty of noise to alert any forest creatures of my presence, I plunge nervously onward. Only a few dozen more yards leads me to the bank of a beautiful mountain creek that meanders beside a high bank, across a shallow riffle, and down into to a pool that disappears beneath a log jam—the gorgeous sort of log jam that in any reasonable trout stream must hold a lunker trout, and which also looks nearly impossible to fish without losing a few flies. Which is to say, the sort of place I could spend an hour fishing at least (and probably lose a few flies). Though it's hard to tell from where I stand, there appears to be another, wider pool below the log jam. The water is very clear. No kale smoothie here. As far as I can see, the stream is only as wide as my fly rod is long, much like the section of Corral Creek I fished in Wyoming. Except unlike Corral Creek, the forest is thick here. The canopy closes completely overhead giving barely a hint of the creek that flows beneath those branches. Fallen trees—and there are many of them—have no trouble spanning the creek.

I take a deep breath. The creek is close enough to the road that it doesn't feel too risky adventuring alone. Plus, the fishing looks promising. I return to the car, don my waders, rig my fly rod, and head back across the clearing into the woods singing and whistling loudly and with my bear spray at my hip. Somehow, however, I don't follow the exact same route. I find my way blocked by thick growth. I whistle more loudly and then glimpse a sudden movement in brambles twenty feet in front of me. I don't get a clear look, but my senses suggest a large mammal moving furtively toward my right.

My heart pounds. My brain tells me it is a deer. My fears tell me it could be a bear. I back away a few steps, grip my bear spray, and inch toward a more open patch of wood. I now spot the more open path I had followed a few minutes earlier, leading to the right along the edge of the gully. I hesitate to proceed. That's also where the large animal seemed to be headed. I look to my left just in time to see a deer no more than a dozen yards away sneaking past me back in that direction. I breath a deep sigh of relief, take my hand off the bear spray, and plunge ahead toward the creek. I find it a few dozen yards downstream of where I had earlier reached it.

Where I hit the creek, it is wide and shallow. I don't see any water immediately around me that looks like it would hold trout. Wading looks easier than cutting through the trees— especially with a fly rod in hand. So I step off the bank and into the water. I turn upstream and as soon as I come around the next bend I see the logjam. From the downstream side, the pool below it looks even better. I approach carefully, and spot a trout just above the riffle at the bottom of the pool. It's over a foot long—a good-sized fish for a stream this small. I am studying it when I spot a second one, almost as big. And then a third, fourth, and fifth fish, all smaller than the first two. My heart is racing again, almost as fast as when the deer crept past me pretending to be a bear. I try to plan an approach that will allow me to get a fly to the fish. Trees close over the stream down to shoulder level.

I'm only twenty-five feet from the fish, but there is no way to cast through the branches. I crouch down low and inch forward very slowly, trying not to spook the fish. The trout don't move and I keep creeping closer until I am out from under the branch. Finally I stop, just barely more than a rod length away. There is still no way to lift my rod, but I can flick a fly ahead of them from here.

I begin to drop artificial nymphs into the pool and drift them along the bottom—a challenging task since I have almost no room to manipulate my fly rod. The largest fish ignores them, but on my third of fourth drift the next biggest one chases. I hook him briefly, but with the forest so close over my head I can't lift my rod to set the barbless hook, and he spits it after a couple seconds. He ignores the next several casts, but I catch one of the smaller trout. It's a Westslope cutthroat, not as colorful as those I had seen below the beaver dam on the remote lake a few days earlier, but still beautiful. I release it and keep fishing. The two bigger fish now ignore the fly altogether. Apparently, they have seen it too many times. I change two more times, trying other imitation nymphs, before I find another they are interested in. I hook the second largest one once more, but again I can't set the hook because of the overhead branches, and again he spits it. I inch closer and get a little more overhead space.

Finally, I get a natural looking drift. I see the trout turn as though to grab my fly. I set the hook, and the fish rolls. I have him on, but realize almost at once that I've hooked him in the tail. I'm able to net him quickly. This one has a deep blood-red belly, and a dark green back. Definitely looks like a male with spawning colors. I take a quick photo of the fish in the water, and release him. His disappears under the bank. Immediately the smaller fish move into his place. What I had suspected earlier now becomes more evident. The largest fish is a female, and she is in spawning mode. She doesn't seem to be feeding. The rest are males, presumably competing for the right to spawn with her. The smaller ones start making their moves on this fertile female. She ignores the young bucks. Then again, she seemed to be ignoring the big one also. A minute later, however, the big one returns, chases the small ones off, and takes his place beside her once again.

I watch the drama for a while: the larger spawning male and female pair, with three smaller males below them hoping for some reproductive action. The large male feeds occasionally as bits of food drift by, but he never moves far from the female, and if the others get too close he turns and chases them off.

Not wanting to upset spawning fish on their redds, I cease fishing and enjoy watching the drama. Then, to avoid any risk of trampling the redd or disturbing the fish further as I move upstream, I step out of the creek onto the bank and work my way through the trees. I stay in the area a little longer attempting to explore both downstream and upstream, but tangles of fallen trees across the creek and thick brush on the banks block my passage in both directions. The fact that spawning cutthroat trout would make a nice meal for a grizzly bear, and that I can't see more than a few dozen yards in any direction—and in places I can barely see a dozen feet—also keeps me from forging a path through the thicker brush. Aware how fortunate I was to have stumbled on the spawning trout and to have watched the drama, I return to the car.

Page 77: Author Matthew Dickerson uses his favorite technique to search for trout on Wyoming's La Barge Creek (part of the Colorado River drainage) near the boundary of the Bridger-Teton National Forest. This stretch of river is not far from the impassable barrier that protects the populations of native Colorado River cutthroat trout being restored to the river from new invasions of non-native fish.

Page 79: As evening falls on Avalanche Lake in Glacier National Park, small native westslope cutthroat rise to the surface to feed on hatching insects. As westslope populations are increasingly threatened by competition, predation, and hybridization from non-native trout species, the future of the westslope species may rest in a few alpine ponds like this one above the reach of invading species.

Page 80: Hybridization. Invasive genes of the introduced rainbow trout have spread farther into the Flathead drainage and the greater Glacier ecosystem than previously thought. How do you spot it? The only reliable answer is genetic studies. However, the late Robert Behnke notes that inland cutthroat trout generally "have no spots or only minute black specks on the top of the head" while on rainbow trout or cutthroat-rainbow hybrids, "the top of the head is heavily spotted" (139). Behnke also describes the westslope cutthroat as having "small, irregularly shaped spots" with few or no spots on the lower front of the body. **Top:** The last and biggest fish landed on a day-long drift down the Middle Fork of the Flathead—and briefly lifted from the water for a quick photo before a gentle release—has the slash mark on the jaw and a lack of spots on the lower front arc of the body suggesting westslope cutthroat. **Below:** This fish, caught three days later and a couple miles upriver, has coloration and spot patterns more characteristic of a rainbow with little or no hint of cutthroat.

Page 81: Top: A beaver dam frames the reflection of two of Glacier National Park's iconic mountains: Longfellow Peak and Heavens Peak. **Below:** Downstream of the dam and below the surface, cutthroat trout in their spawning colors—perhaps blocked by the dam in their effort to migrate upriver—congregate in a small grassy pool in the shadow of a fallen tree.

Page 83: Great Bear Mountain rises from the Flathead National Forest. Drifting the Middle Fork of the Flathead for a day of flyfishing with Glacier Anglers, looking southwest out of Glacier National Park near the village of Nyack, we caught glimpses of the peak. This stretch of river produced several nice trout, but its beauty belied another threat to the ecosystem: a heavily used railroad track that runs along the river carrying fossil fuels. Regular trains could be heard rumbling past throughout the day.

Page 84: A pair of small native westslope cutthroat trout compete for food in Snyder Creek, downstream of Snyder Lake. This water is believed to be above the reach of the many introduced (invasive) species, such as eastern brook trout and rainbow trout that inhabit Lake McDonald (and probably lower portions of this same creek). Small alpine lakes like Snyder Lake, and their little outlet and inlet creeks are protected within Glacier National Park. They are among the best and most important refuges of the westslope cutthroat species.

Page 85: Big Chief Mountain looks down upon the South Fork of the Little Wind River as it flows through an un-named meadow, 10,000 feet above sea level in the Popo Agie Wilderness area of the Shoshone National Forest. Surrounded by and downstream of Loch Leven, Washakie Lake, the South Fork Lakes, and Valentine Lake, this stretch of river was heavily populated with a variety of introduced fish including brook trout and various cross-strains of rainbow and cutthroat trout. Of those, only the cutthroat is native to Wyoming, and even cutthroat are an introduced species in high elevation waters of the Wind River Range.

A curious cub poses for an appreciative audience not far from the top of Sylvan Pass on the western side rim of the Yellowstone Lake drainage. Mother bear was not far off, looking for food—a more difficult task because of the collapse of the cutthroat trout population in Yellowstone Lake resulting from the illegal introduction of invasive Lake Trout.

Snyder Lake on Horseback,
Avalanche Lake at Dusk,
and the Hope of Native Cutthroat

Monday, June 19

My wife Deborah has come to the park for a short visit during my residency. We arise at 6:00 a.m., eat a quick cold breakfast, make lunch, and pack gear for the day. At 7:15 a.m., we walk out the cabin, across the road, and through the woods to the stables of Swan Lake Outfitters which sits in the woods just a short distance up the Sperry Trail. We check in just before 7:30 a.m. I see my name on the reservation at the top of the stack along with our wrangler's name, Rob. I'm looking forward to meeting him, and my horse.

It takes a few minutes to repack lunch and my camera gear into the saddlebags. I load my backpacking fly rod, too, and a couple of small fly boxes, which I have tried to keep with me in my explorations around the park. The folks at the corral give us safety instructions, and then lead us to our horses. Deborah gets a tan horse with a blond mane. His name is Mick. I meet Hooch, my own mount for the day. He is brown with gray dappling on his sides and a white splotch on his forehead. I'd like to call the white patch a "star", which sounds more elegant than "splotch". But the shape of the patch isn't that distinct. I stick with "splotch". His hooves are huge. The name Hooch does not breed confidence; in our safety briefing we were told that alcohol was prohibited on the trips. But though Hooch is the largest horse in the stables, he is mellow and shows no signs of having been nipping from the bottle.

Lastly, we meet our wrangler Rob, and his mount Bandit. Rob is friendly. He is almost thirty. I discover that he is an avid fly fisher, and I'm impressed to learn that he has cast flies in New Zealand, on both the Argentinian and Chilean sides of Patagonia, and also in Alaska. Last summer, he spent a month backpacking in the Wind River Range across the divide from where I was with Phil, Rob, Yuki, and Julia. We talk a lot about fishing, as well as his upbringing on a fruit farm with three sisters whose love of riding meant that Rob spent a lot of time in stables taking care of horses.

We are on the trail before 8:00 a.m. I enjoy the views across the steep Snyder Creek gorge toward Lake McDonald as well as the conversation with Rob, and the two-hour ride passes quickly. As we leave the Sperry Trail and turn onto the narrower and less-traveled Snyder Lake Trail, we ask Rob about bears and the recent closure of Avalanche Lake due to the presence of a grizzly sow and her cub. Avalanche Lake is less than two miles from Snyder Lake by crow flight. Not being a crow myself, those two miles would be impassable for me. Blocking any direct route is a towering ridge extending from the impressive triangular rock spire of the Little Matterhorn (7,886 feet) on the northeast side of Snyder Lake, around to Mount Brown (8,565 feet) to the northwest. That puts the Little Matterhorn more than 2,500 feet above Snyder Lake and roughly 4,000 above Avalanche Lake. Sheer ledges line much of this ridgeline, and though some climbers do summit the Little Matterhorn, there is no trail from the Snyder Lake side. Nonetheless, though grizzly bears are also unable to fly like crows, I suspect they would have far less trouble than I would crossing the terrain that separates us from Avalanche Lake.

Rob reminds us that horses are big animals, even compared with a grizzly—as if I weren't aware of that from my lofty perspective in the saddle. Bears tend to avoid horses. We remember that reassurance when we come upon an area where a grizzly has recently been digging up the ground right next to the trail. Fresh grizzly scat also decorates the ground.

When I begin to see steep rock walls ahead of me as well as to my right and left, I know we are close to our destination. The Little Matterhorn seems to rise even higher. Snyder Lake sits in a steep bowl at the dead end of this cove, surrounded on three sides by rock ledges, falling almost to the shoreline. A beautiful waterfall pours a long distance down an overhanging cliff to my left before hitting the steep slope of scree and cascading down the valley toward Snyder Creek behind me. A few other less spectacular waterfalls also tumble over the rims above us and down toward the lake.

We see all of this, and come to the hitching post before we actually catch sight of Snyder Lake itself. As Rob takes care of the horses, I walk down to the water to scout for a nice area to set up for the day. We have approached the lake from the west. On the south, across a small bridge to our right, a narrow gap of woods separates lake from ridge and offers a place for a wilderness campsite. The north shore looks steeper and is thick with brush. It would be hard to navigate. Across the lake, the eastern shore is also steep. On the southeast, a tumble of rocks from an avalanche stretches from the base of the cliffs below the ridge all the way down to the water. Just north of that grows a steep corridor of trees. Through gaps in the foliage I can see the white of another waterfall cascading down into the lake. I remember that Upper Snyder Lake is at the top of this. There is no marked trail up to it. I've been told that the fishing is better in the upper lake, perhaps because it is deeper or maybe just fewer people fish there.

The lake itself is the smallest I have visited in the park. It is less than three hundred yards long, corner to corner (east to west), and a little over a hundred yards across (north to south) at the widest point. I had imagined a bigger body of water. Snyder Creek flows out of the west side, not far from the hitching post. This is the same creek that flows into Lake McDonald behind the Lake McDonald Lodge. Invasive brook trout inhabit the creek lower down, but they have not made it up into this lake. Like three of the four remote lakes I have visited so far, the outlet is spanned by a narrow footbridge for hikers. We cross to the south shore, and put our gear down at the designated eating area for wilderness campers.

The water is clear, a sharp contrast to near opacity of McDonald Creek. When the wind isn't rippling the surface, I can see the bottom six feet down and fifty feet out. It is flat, and looks thick with silt. From the steep surrounding terrain, I would have imagined the lake much deeper, and with a boulder-covered or gravel-strewn bottom. Fallen trees line the lakeshore near the outlet, but I see no sign of aquatic vegetation. That a glacier-fed lake would have such a silty bottom does not surprise me. That such a small-volume lake would remain so clear when so much silt carries into it does surprise me. My attention, however, is soon diverted from pondering this question. Standing at the wooded shoreline, I soon see fish rising in the shallower water only thirty feet out. They look small—no bigger than the span of my hand. If I could wade out six feet I would easily be able to get an artificial fly out to one of them, despite the line of trees pressing right against the shoreline to hinder my back cast. I wonder if there are bigger fish out deeper, or perhaps on the eastern edge where the stream tumbles in. Or perhaps there is no "deeper".

Deborah joins me at the water's edge, and points out a pair of even smaller cutthroat trout right at our feet, swimming beneath overhanging branches and nipping at insects on the surface. They are so close I could touch them with a stick. In the clear water, I can see parr markings on their sides. I don't have my underwater camera in hand, but just pointing my DSLR down, I'm able to get a few clear photos even when the fish move down to the bottom. Watching more closely, I see that some of them are feeding on the bottom, nosing around for aquatic insects in the soft silt. Others keep nipping something on the surface. It's better and more mesmerizing than an aquarium.

While Rob takes care of the horses, which are being plagued by biting flies, I hike around the small lake alone, taking photos from different angles, trying to get a sense of the size and character of the lake. I keep scouting for fish as I traverse the rocks at the bottom of the steep scree and approach the trees where the waterfall tumbles down from Upper Snyder. Taking into account the possibility of bears, I avoid the thick underbrush. I see no sign of fish, but the lichen on the rocks is beautiful. So is the soundtrack of birds and water.

We also get a soundtrack of other hikers. They arrive in twos and threes, and a few larger groups. They are all talking about the bear they saw down the trail on their way up. Coming on horseback, we were apparently the only ones who missed it. I'm a little disappointed, but I also think back on an earlier morning when I contemplated making the four-mile hike alone. I decide it was wiser that I didn't. One of the hikers also mentions a horse wandering loose down the trail, which sends Rob off in a hurry to retrieve it. I'm glad he succeeds, especially when he returns to tell me Hooch was the guilty party.

Eventually I set up my video camera and try to capture on digital media some of the birds I hear singing around me, or one of the cutthroat rising for a fly. Neither the birds nor the fish cooperate. The clouds, however, continue to swirl around the pointed peaks above me, and so I focus my videoing efforts on mountains, capturing the clouds and the falling water from melting snow and ice.

Only after lunch do I set up my fly rod. By then the fish have mostly stopped feeding on the surface, at least near the shoreline. I fish for a while, but catch nothing. I see only an occasional rise, always well beyond the reach of my casts. After a couple hours, I put away the video camera and hike once again to the other side of the lake, this time with my fly rod. With all the people around, I'm emboldened to venture through the thicker stand of trees to reach the inlet where the stream cascades down from Upper Snyder Lake into Snyder Lake. With a little work, I reach the stream mouth. I test the silty lake bottom with my wading sandals. It is as soft as it looked, and promises to suck me down and never let go, so I decide against wading out. Instead, I balance on a log far enough from shore to cast. I soon discover several small cutthroat hiding beneath the fallen trees, rising now and then to sip something off the surface. I'm able to entice a few out from cover with my royal Wulff, and I land three olive and white cutthroat, all under eight inches. They have the classic spot pattern of the Westlope subspecies. Although I suspect they are adult fish who will grow no bigger than they already are in this small lake with a short growing season, their sides still bear eight or nine faint blue ovular parr markings I would expect on a juvenile fish. They have no hint of red on their bellies like the big spawning males lower down the mountain, but the beautiful light orange slash mark on the bottom of their jaws connects them with their species.

The ride back down goes quickly. We talk more about fishing. When I mention that I'm hiring a guide for a day on the Middle or North Fork of the Flathead, Rob says he'd be happy to join me. We make arrangements for his next day off, exchange phone numbers and e-mails (despite the fact that neither of us has regular access to either), and then Deborah and I head back to the cabin for dinner.

Though we are both saddle-sore from eight miles on horseback, the following morning Deborah and I rent bikes and get on a different type of saddle. We labor up the Going-to-the-Sun Road from the Avalanche Lake trailhead to the famous Loop. There, after a break to enjoy the views, we turn and zoom back down past scores of hikers trudging upward. As we cruise, my eyes are continually drawn further up the verdant river valley to the northwest, along miles of Upper McDonald Creek as it disappears into the unpaved wilderness, toward its headwaters in the snowmelt off West Flattop, Mount Geduhn, and Anaconda Peak. Mixed with my delight at the beauty is also a twinge of regret I will not get a chance to explore that way. Like so many other backcountry lakes and rivers in the park, it will remain in my memory only as a few glimpses, photos, or lines on a map.

I do make one plan for exploration, however. Though I know the creek has a very low population of trout, and thus notoriously poor fishing, I decide I will spend a morning exploring it with a fly rod. I scout out a few likely looking pools, and also consider some of the little waterfall-fed side-streams we cross over where they flow into McDonald Creek. The reality, as I will soon learn, is that much of the hope and future of native Westslope cutthroat trout lies not in the big rivers and lakes down in the valley, but in some of the sources of these little streams: the little alpine tarns and higher elevation lakes spread around Glacier National Park like the twin Snyder Lakes and Avalanche Lake.

Several days later, I speak separately with two cutthroat trout experts. In the morning I meet the National Park Service biologist Christopher Downs for coffee in Columbia Falls. Then I return to West Glacier and connect with USGS biologist Joseph Giersch at the USGS research office, and lastly with USGS biologist Clint Muhlfeld, with whom I spend most of the day on a research-and-teaching field trip with some university students. I question all three biologists about the threats to and future prospects of the native trout of Glacier National Park. Though each has different stories to tell, and varying insights and thoughts related to their experiences, some common threads emerge in these conversations.

With Downs and then Giersch, I speak at length about the impacts of climate change. Glaciers are melting quickly in Glacier National Park. They are just a remnant of what they were a century ago when they gave the park its name. Many expect them to be completely gone by 2030. When they are gone, so too will be the year-round supply of icy cold water that melts off them in the hot summer months, feeding the lakes and rivers and helping keep them full and cool. Combined with a decline in the annual snowpack, climate change is most likely to result in declining summer water levels and increased water temperature.

Giersch is more aware of one aspect of that negative impact than almost anybody. He has been studying two species of stoneflies, the Meltwater Stonefly and the Glacier Stonefly: tiny algae-munching aquatic insects that live almost exclusively in the streams that flow off melting glaciers and permanent snow packs, thriving in greatest numbers within the first few hundred meters below the glaciers. Though they live in streams too small and too close to the glaciers to be of direct importance to feeding cutthroat trout, they are an important part of the alpine food chain, providing the first link from photosynthesizing algae to the animal world. Within a hundred meters of a melting glacier, they can reach densities of about 1,500 per square meter. Larger insects (including species of mayflies) feed on the nearly microscopic stoneflies and in turn become food for birds, rodents, and larger insects. When the glaciers and snow packs have melted away, the prospects for these two small species of stonefly is not good, and an important part of the alpine food chain in Glacier National Park will be gone or greatly diminished. The ecosystem as a whole will be less resilient.

And yet for all of the negative impact of climate change, Downs thought that the population of native cutthroat within Glacier National Park as a whole was well-positioned to adapt to the changes. The waters of the park are protected from development and resource extraction such as forestry and mining. There are no road-building projects. Rivers like Upper McDonald Creek, which I had so admired on my bike trip, flow through largely undisturbed forested wilderness. Compared to much of the country, pollution is minimal. In short, there are few additional stressors other than climate change. There will likely be some rivers or portions of rivers whose temperatures are habitable for trout right now that will become too warm in twenty years, but there will also be some waters currently too cold for ideal cutthroat trout habitat that may become more suitable later. Reduced water flow will likely have an impact also, but the numerous deep lakes provide good summer and winter habitat for trout.

Taken as a whole, Downs suggested that there will be some shifting of cutthroat trout patterns and habitats as climate change continues, but overall, a healthy continuing population is possible.

That outcome, however, depends on keeping the other stressors beside climate change minimal. The most important of the common threads among my conversations with the biologists was a reiteration of what I have heard repeatedly whenever I have explored the plight of native cutthroat: the greatest threat to both native trout species in Glacier National Park is the invasion of non-native trout. Although introduced brook trout are present in some park waters—and though elsewhere in the west they have been devastating to cutthroat populations—they are less of a threat at present in Glacier National Park than either lake trout or rainbow trout. Lake trout, which invaded upriver from Flathead Lake (where they were introduced more than a century earlier) have devastated the bull trout population in the park—once one of the most important remaining refuges and strongholds for bull trout left in the country. Lake trout have completely extirpated the bull trout from eight of twelve lakes on the west slope that held bull trout until just a few decades ago. The efforts to save the populations in the remaining lakes are vital.

In Quartz Lake, where the lake trout invasion was discovered relatively early, before the bull trout were decimated beyond recovery, Downs helped to supervise a lake trout suppression effort which has shown great promise. Nearly all species of salmonids spawn in moving water.[29] Lake trout

---

29 There are some salmonid species—arctic char and sockeye salmon, for example—that have small populations that can spawn in certain lakes with ideal conditions, but even those species primarily spawn in moving water as either anadromous, fluvial, or adfluvial life histories.

are the exception: the one truly lacustrine species of trout or salmon. Although lake trout may move into rivers and streams to feed, or use them to colonize new waters, they live the majority of their lives in lakes, and spawn on shoals as deep as two hundred feet. This is one reason they are not generally available as nutrients to piscivorous mammals and birds, and why—as mentioned earlier in the book—lake trout displacing native cutthroat trout (in Yellowstone Lake, for example) has such a dramatic negative impact on the food chain, reaching far beyond the shores of the lake. By catching one hundred lake trout in Quartz Lake, radio tagging them, and then releasing them, Downs' team was able to identify the most important spawning shoal in Quartz Lake. They then used a two-phase approach of targeted gill-netting first to remove a very high percentage of adult lake trout and then a large number of juvenile lake trout, with very little collateral damage in the form of by-catch of other fish. There is hope that such an approach might work on other lakes where lake trout have found a foothold (though the lake might need to be small enough and with a limited number of spawning shoals in order to be effective.)

Of course even eliminating every lake trout in Quartz lake will not in the long run prove effective if the pathway for more invasions remains open. Thus much of the effort to protect Quartz Lake and the remaining lakes from further invasions has focused on building artificial barriers to block lake trout migration up the streams that connect the lakes to Flathead River, and ultimately to Flathead Lake where the invasion began. And that brought our conversation back to the Hungry Horse Dam. Although Downs agrees that the river fragmentation caused by dams is not ideal, the threat of invasive fish is much greater than any other threat. Thus dams like Hungry Horse or other barriers to migration are vital to preserving the remaining native populations. Even with the dam on the South Fork, Hungry Horse Reservoir with its hundreds of miles of tributary streams provides a long, connected, intact ecosystem with a variety of habitats from the deep lake to mid-sized rivers to small tributary creeks. Since the dam was built before the invasion of lake trout and rainbow trout, that connected system also contains bull trout and a native strain of Westslope cutthroat—but no lake trout, no rainbow trout, and no brook trout.

I spend the rest of the day with Clint Muhlfeld. I listen as he teaches a guest lecture on trout biology and river ecology to a dozen university students on the shore of Lake McDonald. He then leads the students northwest into the Flathead National Forest, where he gives them a chance to take part in his ongoing field research. It is a wonderful example of active learning, and of "doing science." After a description of the project, followed by a safety lesson, the students get into wading boots and troop down to a small brook, about three feet wide, that cuts across a meadow full of wildflowers, tall grass, and the young spruce trees of a forest regenerating after a recent fire. The standing husks of blackened tree trunks bear evidence of the fire, as does the absence of mature living trees.

The brook itself is a tributary of a tributary of the North Fork of the Flathead. It also happens to be an important spawning habitat for both cutthroat trout and bull trout. Over the previous year, Muhlfeld's research team has PIT-tagged several juvenile fish in the stream and surveyed the population of trout. The group of university students in this summer class move up the stream with an electroshocking unit to do a follow-up survey. One student holds a device that scans for the PIT tags. Another carries the electroshocking unit in a backpack and holds the wand in his hand as he moves up the stream. Every few steps he gives a warning and then triggers a shock, which temporarily stuns fish within range. Those following behind catch the stunned fish in a net as they drift downstream. They measure the fish. With the few previously measured PIT-tagged fish they find, Muhfield can later compare the measurements to see how much growth has occurred. They can also get an estimate of how many of those previous tagged fish still remain in the little brook.

It's a fascinating day. To give the university students the fullest chance to be involved in field work and active learning, I remain an observer, photographer, and videographer, while they handle the shocking, the netting, and (under Muhlfeld's supervision) the measuring and recording process. We find mostly juvenile cutthroat fingerlings about twelve centimeters long, but one monster pushes eighteen centimeters— about as big as the fish I saw in Snyder Lake. I think it must be ready to swim down the little brook out into the wide world of the larger creek and maybe even into the Flathead River itself.

Of perhaps greater importance than the dozen and a half little cutthroat, we also capture and release three small juvenile bull trout, around fourteen centimeters in length. There is a bit of irony to this. Though I have fished in rivers in Montana and Alberta where they were present, in my entire life I had previous caught exactly three bull trout: one in south central Washington state, and two in north central Oregon. In two hours of electroshocking, I have doubled my lifetime sightings of wild bull trout. If those three little ones grow, they will become piscivores at the top of the underwater portion of the food chain, feeding on cutthroat trout and whitefish. But in this brook, the little juveniles still have to compete for insects with the cutthroat trout that greatly outnumber them. Evidence of spawning habitat supporting successful reproduction is a hopeful sign for a threatened bull trout, but the presence of lake trout in the reachable lakes means the three bull trout we measured along with their progeny—if they survive to reproductive maturity—may be limited to a fluvial life in the North Fork of the Flathead.

In addition to watching Clint Muhlfeld teach, we get plenty of time together in the car, going to and from the various locations. As we drive, he reiterates what I had heard from Downs about ecological damage and the future threat caused by invasive fish. While Downs focused on the destructive impact of lake trout, Muhlfeld focuses on rainbow trout and hybridization. He is able to elaborate on two things. The first is how the genes of the rainbow trout and the hybrid rainbow-cutthroat—or cut-bow as anglers often call them—are less well adapted than native Westslope cutthroat to these waters in every measure of fitness. The replacement or hybridization of native cutthroat trout genes with invasive rainbow trout genes results in a less resilient ecosystem. Whereas cutthroat trout have myriad different micro-adaptions to different waters across the park, the rainbow trout are generic, coming from a very small and undiverse gene pool.

The second aspect Muhlfeld shares, which has only recently come to light as genetic testing and gene sequencing has become more effective and cost-efficient, is just how far non-native genes have permeated into the gene pool in Glacier National Park waters. Populations of cutthroat trout that he had previous thought unimpacted by rainbow trout genes have been shown—with the genetic testing—to actually be hybrids with some percentage of rainbow trout genes. Essentially, cutthroat populations in any water reachable via upstream migration from the Flathead River will now have some percentage of hybridized genes. And it isn't only rainbow trout that have hybridized with the native Westslope cutthroat in most park waters. Decades ago, before biologists recognized the significance of different subspecies of cutthroat and their specialized adaptations, two lakes in the park had been stocked with non-native Yellowstone cutthroat trout. Whereas the lake trout had to migrate upriver over difficult barriers to invade new lakes, these non-native cutthroat were stocked in higher-elevation headwater lakes, including Hidden Lake near Logan Pass. To reach other waters, they had only to swim downstream.

Only a few remaining high elevation lakes in the park still held unhybridized native strains of Westslope cutthroat. Avalanche Lake, Snyder Lake, and Upper Snyder Lake were three of them. So in some sense, the future of a subspecies lies in those few mountain lakes above impassable falls and barriers, or in Hungry Horse Reservoir and its headwaters. Those little wild Snyder Lake cutthroat trout I had seen, photographed, and in a couple instanced lured to hand with a fly rod and fly, really did represent the hope of their kind.

A couple of days after my visit with the biologists, I take my second hike to Avalanche lake, this time in the evening, with a fly rod, and alone. Well, not quite alone. A steady line of hikers moves in both directions. There are no bears present to close the trail this time, and enough people are around that I'm not at risk of violating the warning signs not to hike alone. I bump into a delightful family of four from Arkansas—Kevin, Jenny, Ella, and Silas—whom I had met the day before when I returned up the Sperry trail to explore Snyder Creek. We strike up a conversation as we ascend one of the park's most popular and most scenic hikes, while Silas (the youngest), makes sure we don't surprise any bears on our hike by repeatedly calling out "Hey bear!" as we walk. By the end of the hike, I realize we have become friends.

I emerge from the heavily wooded trail and onto the shore of Avalanche Lake. Once more, I gaze in awe and delight at the splendor of waterfalls filling a turquoise alpine lake at the bottom of a deep and steep-sided bowl. The sun has already dipped behind the ridge ahead and to my right, which separates me from the pair of Snyder Lakes. The low angle of the evening light accentuates the shadows and textures of the opposite shore: the glittering white of cascading water as it plunges through myriad shades of browns and grays of the bare rock higher up, then on through rich green hues where the trees have successfully colonized the lower slope. On my previous trip to Avalanche Lake, the stiff wind blowing off the snow-covered ridge had chilled me after my sweaty hike, cutting short my stay despite the stunning beauty of the place. Now a much calmer breeze feels cool and refreshing after a hot day. Saying goodbye to my new friends from Arkansas, I work my way around the southeast side of the lake until I come to a place where—stepping or leaping from rock to rock—I'm able to get far enough from the shoreline trees to cast a fly.

A few trout are rising, just at the end of my casting range where a darker blue marks the drop-off from shallow water into the deep unknown. I tie on a dry fly, and manage to entice a few of those cutthroat to take my imitation. None of them are longer than eight inches—roughly the size of the cutthroat I'd found in Snyder Lake—but like the trout in Snyder they are bright and beautiful in their white, silver, and olive green. I think their backs are a darker green than their cousins on the other side of the ridge, though it might be a trick of the fading evening light. More fully aware, now, of how the Westslope cutthroat in those two lakes may be the future of their species, I hold them gently and reverently in the water for a moment, not even taking the time for a photo, and release them, so to speak, "back to the future".

The sun continues its evening path. The shadow of the ridge behind me has almost swallowed the ridge across the lake. Only the very tops of the trio of waterfalls plunging off the ridge to the south still glimmer with reflected sunlight. I glance back toward the trailhead. The other hikers have departed. Despite the earlier crowds, I am now alone at the lake. It will be dark soon. Though some fish are still rising, I turn to depart.

Lake McDonald, McDonald Creek, and a Lone Bull Trout

June 23

My alarm wakes me at 4:30 a.m. I've been thinking about my second visit to the Flathead National Forest south of Glacier National Park a few days ago, and about the fish I saw rising in Hungry Horse Reservoir by the inlet of Emery Creek: the trout I had not been able to entice with a fly.

I've been wanting to cast a fly in Lake McDonald. Unlike Hungry Horse Reservoir, it is no longer a native fishery. Lake trout, brook trout, and rainbow trout (with varying degrees of help from humans) have all invaded its waters. Any remaining cutthroat certainly have rainbow trout genes mixed in. For that reason, it has been a lower priority for me to explore Lake McDonald than many other waters in the park. Also, I have no boat, and the only fish I have seen feeding on the surface have been a hundred yards off shore, far beyond my casting range. Still, it would be a shame to have slept on its shores for four weeks without exploring the lake at least once with a fly rod. I'm curious what I will find if I do.

I think my best chance to find trout in Lake McDonald without a boat will be fishing at a stream mouth, probably early in the morning. I know that many lake-resident fish come in at night to forage by the mouths of streams. Having walked or ridden on horseback much of the length of

Snyder Creek, and having fished in it further upstream and seen where it flows out of Snyder Lake, it would bring a certain closure to my stay to visit the creek's terminus in Lake McDonald.

The air is almost 50° F when I arise. It is the warmest morning of my visit so far. I make a thermos of coffee, but postpone breakfast. By 5:00 a.m. I am standing on the shore of Lake McDonald behind the lodge where Snyder Creek flows in, some four miles downstream of Snyder Lake. Wendell Berry (one of my favorite authors) in his essay, "A Native Hill" (one or my favorite of his essays), writes about the nature of streams. His narrative follows his walk alongside a stream that tumbles down the hillside near his home in Kentucky, and describes arriving at the confluence of two streams: "But the two streams meet precisely as two roads. That is, the stream beds do; the one ends in the other. As for the meeting of the waters . . . the one flow does not end in the other, but continues in it, one with it, two clarities merged without a shadow."[30] Which is to say, when one stream flows into another, it is the terminus of the stream in name only. The same principle must also hold where a stream flows into a lake. The stream bed might come to an end, but the stream does not.

I think about the truth of that. The volume of water pouring down little Snyder Creek, even during spring snowmelt such as I've been observing the past few weeks, feels insignificant compared with that of Lake McDonald, or even compared with Upper McDonald Creek that flows into the lake just a few hundred yards away. The lake swallows up Snyder Creek even more completely than the Upper McDonald Creek would, leaving no discernable trace of it

---

30 Op. cit, 618.

beyond a few dozen yards from the mouth. Yet I know that Upper McDonald Creek is just the joining of hundreds of small creeks like this one, pouring down the slopes of this long valley. Remove all of those tiny creeks and Upper McDonald Creek would cease to exist, as would (eventually) the lake. Also, to the myriad creatures who live in or near Snyder Creek, it isn't insignificant. And to the big fish that come from the lake to feed by the mouth of the creek—the ones I'm hoping to find this morning—it's also not insignificant.

Looking more closely at the mouth of the creek for the first time, the alluvial fan is quite evident: the large wedge of gravel, sand, and sediment that the creek has carried down the mountain over centuries and deposited where the creek levels out and the current slows down upon entering the lake. In the next paragraph of his essay, Berry continues his reflection on the meeting of streams, and gets at one of the fundamental realities of the world we live in: a fact about water, gravity, erosion, and the reasons for this alluvial fan that I begin to wade out on with my fly rod.

> All waters are one. This is a reach of the sea, flung like a net over the hill, and now drawn back to the sea. And as the sea is never raised in the earthly nets of fishermen, so the hill is never caught and pulled down by the watery net of the sea. But always a little of it is. Each of the gathering strands of the net carries back some of the hill melted in it. Sometimes, as now, it carries so little that the water seems to flow clear; sometimes it carries a lot and is brown and heavy with it. Whenever greedy or thoughtless men have lived on it, the hill has literally flowed out of their tracks into the bottom of the sea.[31]

---

31 Wendell Berry, "A Native Hill", 618.

This alluvial fan is not just something that the water carried down the mountain. It is the mountain itself. Or a small part of it. Though, thanks to the protected forests of Glacier National Park, that erosion has not been exaggerated and accelerated by greedy and thoughtless men; it is simply the natural work of the annual melting of glaciers and snow packs combined with the falling of rain.

I walk out onto bits of the mountain that are now bits of the lake bottom wishing for two things. One is a beautiful sunrise. In that, I am not disappointed, though the beauty is in the majestic skyline, cloudscapes, and the alpenglow, its golden hours contrasting with the dark purple shadows, and not in any traditional sunrise hues of pinks, reds, and oranges. Iconic sunrise pinks are not visible down low on the western side of the park behind the row of 8,000 to 10,000-foot peaks. Nonetheless, this sunrise is well worth the early wake-up. The higher slopes are still patched with snow, and clouds look like a whole other mountain range of their own. I am already planning to return tomorrow.

The second thing I wish for—as already noted—is to find some of the lake's bigger fish feeding where the current of Snyder Creek drops off that small alluvial fan into the deep, dark green water. In that I am only partly disappointed. The fish are already rising, just as they had been at the same hour two days earlier at the mouth of Emery Creek on Hungry Horse Reservoir. Some of the heads nipping insects on the surface look much bigger than any trout I have so far seen in the park. They don't belong to little seven-inch creek-resident. Thanks to the way the fan has reached out into the lake, the rising fish are also close enough in to cast to without going deeper than my ankles. My expectations are high.

I look closely. I cannot see any insects coming off the water. Either it is still too dark, or the insects are too small, or both. Yet I know insects are active. Not only are fish rising, but swallows have also awoken early and are busily swooping down low to the water, darting left and right, or occasionally turning suddenly upward and chasing skyward some prey invisible to me. An American dipper—also known as a water ouzel—is also feeding in the lake at the edge of the creek. So this joining of waters really is a place of abundance: a good place for fish. It is someplace special for ecological reasons and not just reasons of my imagination.

Unfortunately, not knowing what the trout are feeding on, I also don't know what fly to use. My fear, since I don't see any insects coming off the water, is that the trout are feeding on tiny emerging midges. They are probably looking for something about a size #30 rising from off the bottom of the lake. The smallest dry flies I have with me are #18, and the smallest midge nymphs I have are #22, which seems tiny to me but they are considerable larger than a #30 midge. For the next half an hour, as the sky steadily brightens, I try several different flies with several different techniques. I drop tiny dry flies on the surface. I drift even tinier nymphs off the edge of the alluvial fan. I lift some flies off the bottom to imitate hatching insects. Nothing works. By 5:30 a.m., the insect hatch, whatever it was, has stopped, or the fish have ceased feeding with the coming of daylight. I shift to casting streamer flies below the surface, stripping them in like little forage fish. That fails also.

By 6:30 a.m., a few other folk have wandered from the lodges and cabins down to the shoreline with cups of coffee. I pack up my rod and head back to my cabin to eat a hot breakfast. Then I head toward Upper McDonald Creek.

It is a nice day to be outside. The sky is brilliant blue with little cloud cover. The forecast had promised a beautiful day, and it does not prove to be a false promise. I hike to a stretch of Upper McDonald Creek that is not right next to a crowded pull-off on the Going-to-the-Sun Road. The water level has dropped so much in the past week it looks like a different river. For a while, I sit in my backpacking chair in quiet and watch the water. I watch a female harlequin duck swim by, her feathers a soft tan and brown with a distinctive white disc where I imagine ears. Her more colorful mate, whom many come to the park hoping to see, having finished its mating purposes, has already departed for the coast.

I also see what seems to be a good mix of gravel riff and softer water, with some structure: fallen trees and gravel bars for habitat. And that eventually prompts me to rig my fly rod. I remind myself once again of what I have read, and have heard from numerous knowledgeable sources including biologists, fellow anglers, and fishing guides: Upper McDonald Creek above the waterfalls is a very poor river for fishing. It has even been described as "sterile". I think that applies to a lack of aquatic insects as well as fish. Indeed, the two are closely related. One question I have is, why? Although the waterfall just above Lake McDonald creates an effective barrier to upstream migration, and thus block a population of adfluvial trout who move into the upper creek to feed but then move back down to the lake in the winter, still I know there are populations of cutthroat trout in both Avalanche Lake and Hidden Lake that feed into Upper McDonald Creek through Avalanche Creek. If Upper McDonald above the falls had a habitat to support it, it would be easy enough—and there has been plenty of time—for it to be colonized by trout coming down from above.

That hasn't happened. So the explanation must lie in the creek itself. Various guesses pop to mind. Every June this creek carries a tremendous amount of silt: the continual melting of the mountains caught up in the net of water. I imagine this silt inundates and buries the would-be eggs of the benthic invertebrates as well as trout. Fausch writes about the temperature extremes and fluctuations in rivers fed mostly by runoff from rain and melting snow rather than from the aquifer. In reference to rivers flowing through granite and hard rocks, with little topsoil, he writes, "When the snows melt . . . the water will move quickly through the shallow soils and drain off the bedrock into the stream channel, creating pulsed floods but leaving little groundwater to supply flow later. . . Because there is little stable input of groundwater, stream water temperatures. . . will change rapidly during floods, creating stressful conditions for invertebrates and fish."[32] It sounds like a plausible explanation for the sparsity of fish here. Except the nearby Middle and North Forks of the Flathead, at a cursory glance, come out of the same mountain ranges and have a similar annual June flood regime. Perhaps the reasoning lies deeper, below the surface.

Whatever the reason, my expedition provides further evidence of what I have been told. After some time writing, I get out my fly rod and work a couple hundred yards of river casting to several spots that look likely: seams between fast water and slow, shelves off gravel bars, tops and tail-outs of pools, and all around fallen logs. I don't see so much as a shadow of a fish. I also see no insect activity. No aquatic invertebrates rise off the surface, and none of the rocks I overturn in the water have any signs of life. So it is no wonder

---

32   Fausch, 52.

I have found no fish here. Not that the river is completely sterile. I spot an American Dipper diving underwater by a log on one shoreline. It is obviously eating something. I've also seen a few ducks and sandpipers feeding along the shore. I even see an occasional insect-eating bird swoop out from the shoreline and grab something out of the air. Still, the only wilderness river I can remember with so few signs of aquatic life was a river in Alaska flowing right off a glacier and so full of silt it was the color of wet concrete.

Thus despite how beautiful this creek is, and how clear and clean it runs now that the snow melt has subsided—despite the wilderness character of the water and the protection from upstream logging, mining, or development—the population of cutthroat trout is small. I remember one guide saying that there were a few small pockets where trout lived, but that it could be a long distance between them. I make one final effort to work upstream and look for another possible holding place for cutthroat. I come upon a huge old tree down in the river. A mound of soft silt has piled up behind it, three feet higher than the river bottom and fifteen feet long. One step on the very edge warns me that if I attempt to continue I'm likely to get stuck. I skirt around this impressive underwater silt-mound, and navigate along the log instead.

I wonder how long this tree has been here. One year? Two? Five? The impressive volume of silt behind it is yet another reminder of just how much of the mountain is melted in the river. I also remember my time in Alaska two years ago sitting beside that glacial river talking about the importance of fallen trees in streams, and referencing Fausch's book *For the Love of Rivers*. I was co-teaching with my friend and co-author David O'Hara a Middlebury College summer class: "Alaska and its Char: Essay Writing and Ecology". We used Fausch's book as a text not only because of the depth of knowledge and insight into trout and river biology and ecology, but also because of the beautiful writing. Fausch elucidates the intersection of forest and stream in a single cohesive ecology. One aspect of the interaction of wood and water is how important it is to have a population of trees that die (or get blown over) and can fall into those rivers. Fausch and colleagues did one pioneering study on some alpine streams in Colorado where logging practices a century earlier had removed all the trees on the hillside. Although forests had grown back since, they hadn't been around long enough for mature trees to die. All the trees were relatively young. Their experiment involved putting logs into certain stretches of the stream, and then comparing stretches with logs to those without. They revisited these streams up to eight years later and continued to collect data. The results were telling. Logs in the stream increased trout counts by 50 percent.[33] The logs create pools and habitat both upstream and down—places of shelter, cooler water, and greater availability of food. In other words, it is more than just the shade provided by riparian corridor that is important to streams, and the protection of the streambank against erosion provided by the root systems; even the natural deaths of trees in a forest stream helps the aquatic life. The implications of this study are that activities such as logging and roadbuilding that eliminate the riparian trees and prevent logs from falling into the streams will reduce trout populations significantly.

At midday I head back to the cabin for lunch and to write. As afternoon rolls on, clouds roll in and the breeze shifts to the north. Promised warmth never comes. In the evening I pick up Peter Wohllenben's *The Hidden Life of Trees*, a recent birthday gift to me from my wife. I've been

---

33 Fausch, 73.

reading it during my time at Glacier National Park. I am up to Chapter 18, "The Forest as Water Pump", which by coincidence is about how important of forests are to the streams that flow through them. Wohlleben makes an observation similar to that of Fausch:

> The importance of trees for streams continues even after death. When a dead beech falls across a streambed, it lies there for decades. It acts like a small dam and creates tiny pockets of calm water where species that can't tolerate strong current can hang out... Mud and floating debris drop to the bottom of the tiny dammed pools, and because stream flows are so low, it gives bacteria more time to break down harmful substances.[34]

I saw that in action on the Upper McDonald—thanks in part to a protected forest managed as wilderness where the riparian buffer is allowed not only to grow, but to grow old and die, and topple where it dies. Whatever the ultimate cause of the sterility of this river, it cannot be blamed on the lack of trees. The river is full of them: individual trees toppled from the shoreline as well as big log jams. Such habitat is one of the most valuable parts of the wilderness character of Glacier National Park.

Several years ago, my good friend (and co-author of three books) David O'Hara introduced me to the phrase "fish porn." It is an appropriate term, but not a complimentary one. It refers to a particular genre of fishing media, usually a photograph of somebody holding a very large fish (with a pose and camera angle designed to amplify even further the size of the fish). The purpose of fish porn is to titillate and arouse. It is designed not to reflect love, but to incite lust. It is

---

34 Peter Wohlleben, *The Hidden Life of Trees: What They Feel, How They Communicate*, (Vancouver: Greystone Books, 2015), p. 110.

about making somebody want something. Like other forms of pornography, it is exploitive.

Since hearing the term, I've been particularly cautious in my own writing about trout and fly fishing—especially fishing that involves travel—to avoid producing more fish porn. Rather than a brief mention of a place in order to exploit a few fish, I'd rather have the fish, as well as the activity of fly fishing that brings me into contact with those fish. I'd rather become a medium for bringing myself and my readers into meaningful contact with the place: for sharing both knowledge about and delight in the place itself (and not just seeing the place as a location to catch fish.)

One of the elements of Wendell Berry's essay "A Native Hill" I find so beautiful and compelling is that it takes place in a setting he knows well. The central upland hill in Kentucky is Berry's native land. The river at the bottom of the hill "lies within a hundred steps of [his] door." All his grandparents and great-grandparents had lived within about four miles of Port Royal and "left such memories as their descendants have bothered to keep."[35] Berry's writing—his fiction and poetry as well as his essays—is placed-based writing at its best, growing out of attentiveness, knowledge, memory, and intimacy. For the most part, my biweekly outdoors columns in the *Addison County Independent* focus on Addison County. It is a choice, not only because it is relevant to the interests of readers who live there, but also because it is the land I know the best. The discipline helps me to be present, and to avoid the sort of travel writing that can turn quickly into fish porn.

Yet for all the value of rootedness, there is also something valuable—or so it seems to me—in exploring new places. More specifically, there is value in the practice of

35 Wendell Berry, "A Native Hill", 601.

attentiveness needed to be truly present somewhere unfamiliar. I have found the art and discipline of fly fishing to be one of the best ways for me to practice that attentiveness. Listening, learning, and writing is another. In her book, *Braiding Sweetgrass,* Robin Wall Kimmerer describes an experience she had during a period of her life when she temporarily found herself living in a different part of the country: a region where the native trees and flowers and insect species were largely unfamiliar to her. While teaching a biology class to some pre-med students, she led a three-day field trip into the Smokey Mountains. She describes beautifully the epiphany that came to her at the end of that trip.

> I had been fooling myself that I was the only teacher. The land is the real teacher. All we need as students is mindfulness. Paying attention is a form of reciprocity with the living world, receiving the gifts with open eyes and open heart. My job was just to lead them into the presence and ready them to hear. On that smoky afternoon, the mountains taught the students and the students taught the teacher.[36]

Kimmerer is a wonderful place-based writer, and her knowledge of and attentiveness to her native heritage as well as to the lands where she has lived is part of what makes her writing so compelling (in addition to the beauty of the prose itself.) She writes about home in the deepest emotional and ecological sense of that word. Yet even Kimmerer finds value in visiting the unfamiliar landscape herself, as well as in leading others there with her. Her example is not unlike that of Wendell Berry, who in addition to essays, poems, and novels about Kentucky, has also written about visiting Peru and spending time with potato farmers in the Andes.

---

36   Robin Wall Kimmerer, *Braiding Sweetgrass*, 222.

So I make it my job also, whether writing about the familiar or the new, to be present and ready to hear: to come with open eyes and open heart for the gifts of creation. My goal is to bring my mindfulness as a listener, and as a writer to invite others into the presence of the places I have spent time. When work takes me places like Wyoming, Maine, Alaska, or (as it has right now) to Glacier National Park I take the chance to share those experiences with my Vermont readers, doing my best to be as attentive to the place as I can. I think that desire to approach—as much as is possible in a visit of only one month—a practice of "being present" (with even a hint of rootedness), leads me to give extra attention to the lakes and rivers closest to my cabin. I don't give up on finding a trout in McDonald Creek. I also realize that whether I find a native fish, an invasive fish, or none at all, I will pay attention to what I do find; I will seek to listen and hear.

The day after my early morning fishing in Lake McDonald and the mouth of Snyder Creek, and my first flycasting excursion on Upper McDonald Creek, I repeat my earlier morning excursion to the little creek mouth behind the lodge. Indeed, I repeat almost the identical experience: the solitude of being the first to come to the lake shore, the beauty of an alpine sunrise, watching fish feed in the stream mouth, attempting to catch the fish, and failing. Except on the second morning I don't bother documenting it on film. Over the next four days I make four more visits to various locales on McDonald Creek. I have two spots in particular circled on my mental map: one I heard about from a park ranger, downriver of the lake; another, suggested by a fisheries biologist, upriver of the lake but below the impassable barrier of the waterfalls.

One morning after a late and leisurely breakfast, I drive to Apgar on the outlet end of Lake McDonald. I have a newspaper column due for my paper back in Vermont, and I spend the morning writing it at a table at the iconic Eddie's Cafe and Mercantile in Apgar—paying for my use of the table by buying first a coffee and then some huckleberry pie and ice cream. I finish the pie and ice cream, and also get my column submitted thanks to the small zone of cell phone service. I head next door to the Apgar Education Center where I lead a two-and-a-half-hour lunchtime workshop on creative writing with a focus on narrative non-fiction nature writing. The group is enthusiastic. We spend time discussing "A Native Hill." I share some goals and principles of narrative essays, look at examples from the essay of how Wendell Berry accomplishes these goals, and then I send the attendees out with a writing assignment. Later, I drive beyond Apgar toward West Glacier, and down a side road toward Quarter Circle Bridge which crosses McDonald Creek just above its confluence with the Middle Fork. Once more I am drawn to a confluence. What are the stories here? How do these waters play into the story of the native cutthroat trout that still inhabit these waters? Or of the bull trout?

I park the car and walk out onto the bridge where I just stand and watch the water for a while. The Middle Fork of the Flathead is just a long stone's throw downriver from the bridge. A boat with two anglers moves out of the Flathead into the mouth of McDonald Creek. The anglers take a few casts, then turn back into the current and float away. I look upriver, downriver, toward both banks. Mostly I look straight down toward the bottom of the deep channel below me, trying to spot a monster fish hugging the bottom. Twice I see the shadow of something big slip in and out of sight. One shadow looks thirty inches long or more. I think it must be a big bull trout, but I am not sure. I gaze toward that spot for several more minutes but see no other signs. A smaller fish rises by the western shore in the eddy behind a rock.

Other than one or two little rises, nothing is happening on surface. I tie on a streamer fly and fish off the bridge, looking for flashes or follows. I don't see anything. If my fly attracts the attention of any fish, I have no evidence of it. To my dismay I've become a bridge fisherman, which is something I have always disdained. I don't want to be seen. I look nervously about for cars, but I have the spot to myself. Eventually I leave the bridge and walk down the shore to the bank of the Middle Fork. There is a long seam where the current of the Flathead sweeps past an eddy and backwater against the near shore on the upriver side of the confluence. Unfortunately, the trees and bank make it next to impossible to get a fly out into it without losing the fly. A short distance upriver from the confluence I find another seam beyond an outcropping point. Stripping my streamer from the current back into the slack water, I feel a sharp tug and set the hook. I play the fish. I can tell from the feel that it isn't huge. It gets close and I see a trout a little over a foot long. When I lead it to shore and net it, I am surprised to discover it is a bull trout. Careful to leave the fish in the water, I gingerly unhook it and release it quickly, snapping a couple photos as it swims away.

I have caught my first Glacier National Park bull trout—the first I have ever caught in Montana, and only the fourth I have caught in my life. It will also prove to be my only bull trout of my visit. I think again of its scientific name: *Salvelinus confluentis*. Though I have not studied Latin, I know what the name indicates. It is the char that lives at the confluence of waters. So this fish is aptly named.

I think again of the Wendell Berry passage about the meetings of streams.

I cast for a while longer, but lose my streamer in the tall grass on the steep bank behind me. I head back to the bridge with a new heavier fly to get it deeper, and cast some more. A park ranger comes by to check on me. I can tell from his eyes that he is looking over my equipment to make sure I'm not doing anything illegal. He might have been checking for live bait or treble hooks. I'm not sure. I was fly fishing. He asks if I'm planning on keeping any. I tell him I'm not. He wonders how I'd land a fish if I hooked one from the bridge. It's a very good question—one that I've considered myself when disdainfully watching others fish from bridges. And because I have wondered that, I had scoped it out carefully before I took my first cast. I have a net on my back and there is a path to the shore right beside the bridge. Without hesitation I point to it, and with full truthfulness tell him that was my plan. I don't have waders on, but I mention I had thought about wading. Another flag goes up. He makes sure I don't have felt soles. They are illegal in the park because of the risk of carrying invasive plants. I don't have felt soles, I tell him.

As he drives away, I'm curious what drew him down the road to check on me. Was it one of the passing cars that called in a concern? If so, why? I wonder if he knows something I don't know—like maybe there really are some big *S. confluentis* around this confluence. Maybe he was protecting them, making sure I wasn't targeting them. If that were the case, he might not tell me so because he might not want me to know that there were bull trout there. Maybe he just happened to be passing by, and it was just a routine random check. I don't ask, but I later wish I had. In any case, I don't mind. I'm glad to see that the park is protecting its native fish. I'm always happy to see wardens or their equivalent on patrol.

After the ranger leaves, I pack up my gear and depart. I go only as far as the next bridge upriver in Apgar, where Camas Road crosses McDonald Creek just five hundred yards downriver of Lake McDonald. I park the car and walk out onto the bridge. I look upriver and down. At least a half dozen anglers are fishing. Most cast from the shore, but two are wading. Only one is fly fishing. The rest are casting metal lures with spinning rods. Several more observers watch from the shore. I watch from the bridge for twenty minutes. I see no fish in the water. I see no anglers land any fish. A small number of mayflies and caddis flies – maybe one per minute – come off the water. I see no trout rising for them. I see no swallows feeding on them either. The lack of swallows is an even more sure sign to me that there is no significant hatch taking place. I decide not to bother fishing, and instead just enjoy watching the river and the stories playing out on the shore. I talk with the fly fisher as he comes off the water. He didn't even get a strike, he tells me.

As I turn to leave, a car stops on bridge. The driver asks us how the fishing is. When the angler answers that he hasn't caught any, the man in the car mentions seeing several fish right under the bridge on Upper McDonald Creek between the lake and the falls. I'm always skeptical when I hear something like that unless I hear it from somebody I know and trust. It isn't from any suspicion that somebody is trying to fool me, but simply doubt that the average person knows anything about fish. I've been sent on too many wild goose chases by well-meaning people claiming to have seen large numbers of trout somewhere.

I'm heading that way anyway, however. I drive along the lake and onto North Lake McDonald Road. Twenty-five minutes later I park beside the only car bridge over Upper McDonald Creek. For the third time this evening, I stand on a bridge over some portion of the creek. There are no insects coming off the water, but it doesn't take me long to spot the fish the man had been talking about. There are, indeed, a large number of them swimming in the current almost directly below me. They are stacked up over a shallow gravel bar. They are quite big. Some are larger than anything I have caught in my visit to the park. They are not trout, however. I recognize them instantly as suckers. Had anybody in the park mentioned suckers at any point, I probably would have been expecting that. More often than not, when a non-angler tells me they stood on a bridge over a trout stream looking down at big fish, I discover that the fish are suckers. Every now and then, however, they really are trout.

These suckers are densely populating a gravel bar in the middle of the river, covering a space forty feet wide and ten feet upstream. The density of the fish suggests spawning behavior. This is soon confirmed when three of them (presumably all males) all get very close on top of a fourth one (the female) which starts shaking. This natural reproduction is a good sign of a healthy ecosystem. It's also fun to watch these fish propagate their species. But my thoughts soon turn to the big trout I have caught in Vermont and Maine feeding below spawning suckers. Sucker spawn, like salmon spawn, provide a good source of easy protein for a hungry trout that suck up the eggs that shake loose in the current before settling to the bottom. We are close enough to Lake McDonald that not only cutthroat trout but also bull trout or lake trout might be up in this creek feeding on the eggs. I go to the downstream side of the bridge and look into the water for evidence. I see many swirling shadows from sunlight on green water. Even with my polarized glasses, the creek is too deep, swift, and dark here to see any fish on the bottom. If there are big trout feeding on the eggs, I don't spot them. I take a few casts, but don't get any strikes. I put my fly rod away, and get out my GoPro instead. I try to take some video of the spawning suckers. But the water is too silty to capture video from more than a few feet away, and the suckers won't let me get within a few feet.

It is getting dark. I head back to my cabin, but return a day later for a longer excursion. I fish my way upstream almost to the falls. Then I wade my way downriver all the way to the mouth of the lake—something that would have been impossible in the high water a week earlier. Finally I see fish. A few stray fish are rising just off the river mouth, feeding on some sort of insect. A stiff wind is blowing off the lake into my face, making casting a challenge. The lake waves battle with the river current, which make wading difficult. I try to wade out closer to the rising fish, but when the water level rises above my belt and I feel the current pushing firmly on the backs of my legs—and I'm still too far away to cast to the rising fish—I turned around.

I've visited four spots on McDonald Creek with a fly rod—two above the lake and two below. I fished three of them, one of them being a long stretch at the bottom of Upper McDonald Creek from the falls all the way to the lake. The only fish I caught was a small bull trout, which really came out of the Middle Fork above the confluence, and not out of McDonald Creek itself. Still, the presence of the bull trout as well as the spawning suckers provide some encouragement. Though the lake trout have extirpated them from eight lakes and cut them off from an adfluvial life history, at least they are holding on in the rivers. My trip is almost over, but when I depart Glacier National Park, the mystery of those trout rising at dawn will haunt me for months. So will the trout rising off the mouth of McDonald Creek which I couldn't reach with my flies. So, too, will the thought of the thirty-inch long bull trout that I might or might not have seen under a bridge at the bottom of the creek.

A Day in a Driftboat,
An Afternoon Jaunt with Ranger John,
and Two Forks of the Flathead[37]

It is noon on Sunday, the first day of my last week in Glacier. It is after my first failed attempt at fishing Lake McDonald at the mouth of Snyder Creek, but prior to my failed attempt to catch trout in Lake McDonald at the mouth of Upper McDonald Creek. I connect with Ranger John Ceballos in front of the cafés and gift shops in Apgar. I had met John at the end of my first week in the park when he came to one of the presentations I made as the artist-in-residence. He introduced himself by telling me he had grown up in Middlebury, Vermont, and that his father read my newspaper columns. I felt validated as human. Then he invited me to go fishing with him. I felt thrilled as an angler.

It's crowded and it takes time to find a place to park. I transfer my gear to John's Subaru, help him strap a canoe onto the roof, and we are ready to roll. We take off northward, past Fish Creek and up the Outer North Fork Road. It's my third trip along this route, but when we climb that first hill on the northwestern corner of Lake McDonald, and I look out over the lake at the famous Rocky Mountain skyline of Glacier National Park, I'm still in awe.

We proceed out of the park, across a bridge over the North Fork of the Flathead, and into the Flathead National

---

37   An earlier and shorter version of this chapter first appeared in the Addison Independent, June, 2017, as part of a four-part series on Glacier National Park that was awarded the first place for best sports column (weekly newspaper category) in the 2017 *New England Newspaper and Press Association* (NENPA) annual competition.

Forest. As we drive, I look at maps. Our plans are fluid. John has explored a lot of trout water in his four years as ranger, but he's always interested in exploring new waters. We both want to start by finding a place to wade. Though there is still plenty of snow left in the mountains, the peak of snow-melt and runoff is past. Water levels have dropped and this river looks fishable. John says that the further north we go, the better the fishing is likely to be. He also thinks that the mouth of a creek flowing in from the west would be a good choice. We might even try fishing up a tributary creek as well as in the North Fork itself. Thinking again how much I like confluences, I concur. He has a few ideas of forest service access areas on the west side of the river where the fishing might be productive. He names one. I don't know enough to disagree, so we make it our plan. Along the drive we talk about Middlebury, people John went to high school with and families we both knew. Conversation turns next to his early experiences fishing in Vermont, which were for pike in Otter Creek. He didn't really take up fly fishing for trout until he moved west.

He speaks also of his enjoyment of being a park ranger in such an unspeakably beautiful place. His job involves a lot of educating and interacting with the public. He delights in sharing what he loves with a curious and engaged audience—often younger people learning about important ecological concepts. I can't resist asking him about stupid things visitors to the park occasionally do. He has plenty of those sorts of stories to tell, many involving bears. Some guests have never experienced real wild places before. They have an impression of the whole park as a sort of big zoo, and they think the rangers have a schedule for the animals, and control where they are going to be at what times. This gives a whole new connotation to their question, "Where should I go to see bears?"

Most of the foolish things visitors have done involve attempts to treat wild animals as cuddly tame pets. Just a few days earlier, when the Avalanche Lake Trail had to be closed, some visitors had gotten so close to bears they had forced the bears out into the water. A situation with bears feeling threatened could easily have turned out differently, though in this case, thankfully, it didn't. Many other serious accidents occur around waterfalls, which are abundant in the park. For the most part, however, visitors to the park are respectful, knowledgeable and appreciative. John also talks about living in the Columbia Falls area. Living near Glacier National Park and the Flathead National Forest is wonderful for people who love the outdoors. At times, though, he has felt a little out of place in the community. To my surprise, I learn that among many locals there is an attitude of resentment because of the restrictions related to land use necessary to preserve the wilderness character of the park. Locals want to be able to drive their ATVs and shoot their guns around the park. Both of those activities are prohibited.

I also learn from John that the entire annual budget for the million-acre national park with hundreds of employees is only twelve million dollars. He was once doing an educational presentation for some students from a local school. One student—perhaps from a family that resented Glacier National Park—suggested this was an excessive amount of money to spend on a park. John put that into context for the student by pointing out that it is less than what many good receivers in the NFL make per year. The annual salary of an NBA star, Cy Young Award-winning pitcher, or Super Bowl winning quarterback might actually be double the entire annual budget for the park. All the staff salaries, research costs, road work, building repairs, and work of conservation, preservation, and restoration, all must be done with that budget. Thus a lot of important conservation and research projects are underfunded.

As we drive through a forested part of the road, a large white owl soars over the road in front of us and disappears into the trees. We both think it looked like a snowy owl, but in summer months they would typically be found only much further north, in or near the arctic. Though not completely unheard of, a snowy owl in the lower forty-eight in the summer is quite surprising. Yet neither of us can think of any other large white raptor that might be mistaken for a snowy owl.

As we drive pass Polebridge and the northwest entrance to Glacier National Park, we begin to look more closely at tributary creeks that pass under the road. Several look promising, but I have no real knowledge of the area. Eventually we arrive at the USFS Ford River access road, that crosses over Tepee Creek. John pulls in to take a look. He has fished here in the past with some success. Though the water is higher now than when he had been here before, it looks low enough to fish. We park the car atop a high bank overlooking the river and rig up our rods. The river flows eastward here for a short distance, so the view downstream across the emerald water is straight into the park. Glacier's famous northern peaks are still splotched with snow. The sky is blue and cloudless. A few kayaks and inflatable rafts drift past us, and a car or two wanders behind us along the dirt road. Overall, though, it is quiet, remote, and beautiful.

And no fish are biting. We work our way slowly upriver to the mouth of Tepee Creek. Each of us thinks we might have gotten one strike, but we never really have anything on the other end of the line. After an hour and a half, we pack up and drive downriver to the village of Polebridge, along a poorly marked dirt road over an old bridge, and back into Glacier National Park. Just upriver of the bridge over the North Fork near the kiosk and entrance to the park, Bowman Creek flows into the North Fork. It's another confluence, another place to fish. We park behind the kiosk and walk down to Bowman to sit on the bank and eat cherries and enjoy a cold drink. From our perspective looking down the small creek, the upstream side of the confluence is the place to be. Getting there requires some adventurous bushwhacking. I send John first in case we run into bears hiding in the bushes we whack. Eventually we find ourselves standing on the bank of the North Fork. John begins to fish seriously right where we are. I feel called by the confluence and I starting working my way down the shoreline.

Eventually I arrive, and the spot looks great. Bowman Creek splits around a gravel bar as it flows into the North Fork. The current flowing around both sides creates a lovely pool of soft water behind the bar, with forty to fifty feet of nice seam line on one side, and twenty more on the other, plus the soft water in the pool itself. I wade across one side of the current and out to the gravel island. The water is deep, but with little current, so I'm comfortable getting out to my belt line. I take a few casts with an attractor-pattern dry fly and a nymph dropper, but it doesn't attract any attention. My expectations for catching a trout are low, but I keep working. I switch to a streamer fly I tied with green and white buck tail and a little splash of red yarn. I think it makes a good imitation of a little trout. I begin on the upriver side, casting into the swift current and stripping out through the seam into the soft water. The technique works, and over the next half hour as I work slowly down toward the tail of the pool I land four cutthroat trout, all about twelve to fourteen inches long. A few others strike my fly but manage to get off.

At the tail of the pool my fly draws several flashes, and I realize as I wade out a little that it is quite deep. I can't see the bottom. Wanting to get a fly down a little farther, I remove the buck-tail streamer and tie on a heavily weighted wooly bugger. I cast it out into the current and swing it back through the seam, letting it slide downstream so the weight of the fly can sink it. When it feels like it's down deep, I strip it back in slowly. I feel a hard hit and set the hook. Whatever I have is a good fighter and smart enough to get out into the current. I reel it in to find a mountain whitefish, another cold-water species native to these waters. It is good to see it in here. The smaller whitefish are good forage for big bull trout. They are also part of the important species diversity in these waters.

I cast the wooly bugger some more but to no avail. So I snip it off and decide to go back to a dry fly. I tie on a big elk hair caddis that will float high in the turbulent water. I take a few casts out onto the edge of the current and get no strikes. So I just lay the fly out onto the calm water in the center of the pool. A large shadow flashes up from deep in the dark green water and slams the fly. I'm able to set the hook, and after a good fight I soon land the fattest fish of the day: a 15-inch cutthroat that rose from the bottom of the pool to hit my caddis imitation.

John soon joins me. I let him have the hole and I explore a few dozen yards up Bowman Creek. I catch one more trout behind a rock near the shore. Then we finally pull ourselves away from the hole, scramble and whack our back through the thick bushes and alders, past all of the bears that stay hidden as we pass. We hop into the car and drive seven more miles up a bumpy gravel road to Bowman Lake. I comment that the unpaved dirt road—which I am now traveling for the third time—is in rough shape. The potholes threaten to shake the canoe off the car. Not wanting to insult a Glacier National Park ranger, I don't say aloud what I'm thinking: that Yellowstone National Park doesn't have any roads this poorly maintained. I do, however, comment aloud that the Inner North Fork Road from here down to Camas is no longer a through-road. It is closed because of some repair issues.

John has clearly wondered the same things. He does not work in the park year-round, and this is only his fourth year as an interpretative ranger. He doesn't know all of the internal or external politics. The closure of the road to Camas, and the bad shape of the Bowman Lake road might be because of funding challenges. As we have already noted, $12 million is a woefully small budget for a million-acre park with hundreds of staff that will service over 600,000 visitors and nearly 80,000 overnight guests just in the month of June.[37] In July, when the Going-to-the-Sun road is open, and kids have the whole month off from school, the number of visitors is much higher. The lack of funding is the only explanation needed. But John notes that there are also possible advantages to the poorly maintained road. Even with the rough road, Bowman Lake received enough visitors today to fill the parking lots. Seven miles of rough road may help dissuade even greater crowds. Likewise, closing a portion of the Inner North Fork road so that it is not a throughway may dramatically cut the traffic and help to preserve the wilderness character of the park, cutting down on numbers of casual tourists.

Whatever the reasons, our teeth rattle for twenty minutes, but the canoe stays on. We park, unload the canoe and paddles and fly-fishing gear. Then we spend the last two and a half hours of daylight in one of the most scenic places in

---

37   https://irma.nps.gov/Stats/SSRSReports/Park%20Specific%20Reports/Park%20YTD%20Version%201?Park=GLAC   August 1, 2017.

Glacier National Park. The water, with a tint of glacial green, at moments as calm as glass, reflects the park's famous northern spires and jagged peaks. Thrushes sing to us from the woods. Small cutthroat trout rise in patches of calm water.

But, as it turns out, not so many or so big that we actually catch any.

The lake is several miles long, and we never get out of site of the western shore where Bowman Creek flows out. For much of the evening, all around the outlet, a lot of small fish rise for mayflies that are falling to the surface to lay eggs. Unfortunately, we see very few big cutthroat rise, and those that do are sporadic and spread far apart. Though we land no fish, it doesn't matter that much to me. I had already caught plenty for the day. Though we happen to have fly rods with us, and we cast them from time to time, both of us think of this excursion as a sunset canoe trip on a beautiful lake, watching the alpenglow on distant snow-covered pinnacles that rise like crow's beaks pecking the sky. In that, we are not disappointed at all.

It is midnight by the time I get back to my cabin. I had come a long way to meet somebody from Vermont with the same passions for natural beauty, fly-fishing, and education. In the midst of many wonderful days, it was one of the very best.

Despite my late arrival back at the artist's cabin, I am up early the next morning. I have scheduled a drift trip with the Glacier Anglers outfit along the Middle Fork of the Flathead River that forms the park's southern boundary with Flathead National Forest. Combined with my evening outing to the North Fork, this will help provide a bigger picture of two major forks of the Flathead and the park's south and west boundaries. It will also be a first-hand experience with cutthroat trout in a carefully managed water. Rob, the Swan Mountain Outfitters wrangler who brought me by horseback to Snyder Lake, has the day off. He has made plans to join me. Having his company will be more fun. Just about the time I finish my coffee and I'm packed to go, Rob shows up at the cabin. We load his gear in my rental truck and head out of the park, arriving at Glacier Anglers on the outskirts of West Glacier a little before 8:00 a.m. I get another coffee at the kiosk out front, and then we head inside to check in. When all the paperwork is filled in, we meet our guide Blake. To make lunch and transportation more convenient, Blake has paired up with Mark, another guide, and his two clients. Around 8:30 a.m., we hop into the eight-passenger vehicle for a twenty-minute drive up-river to our put-in point for a seven-mile drift.

On the drive, I learn from Blake and Mark that this is the first day of the season for floating this river with clients. It took until late June for the river to get low enough to fish. Fortunately, though it's the first day with clients, Blake had scouted it the day before—and caught fish. I also discover that Blake grew up one town away from the village in Maine where I went to kindergarten and where my brother now lives. For the second time in two days, I think that as big as Glacier National Park is, the world really is small. Blake went to the same prep school with daughters of our friends who live in a village of five hundred people two thousand miles away to the east. He is still a college student at Westminster College in Salt Lake City, Utah—taking his time finishing. He goes to school in the fall, but takes off the winter and spring to be a professional mogul skier. I learn that Mark has also guided in Alaska and on the Yellowstone River. He and Rob have both fished Patagonia. I enjoy listening to them swap stories. I'm equally excited to learn that Mark remembers reading my recent story in *The Drake*.

We put into the river at the Cascadilla Creek boat launch off US-2. Blake starts me with a pair of dry flies. Rob gets a dry fly with a nymph dropper. As we drift down the first section of river, we focus on pockets behind shoreline boulders and fallen logs. Blake says there is good fishing in these spots later in summer, and he caught some fish on his scouting mission the day before. On this morning, however, they don't produce. For the first two hours, I don't get a single strike. Rob manages one soft hit, but he doesn't get a good set and isn't able to bring the fish in.

Despite the minimal action, I enjoy the morning. Peaks on both sides of the river rise over 7,000 feet. The tallest are on the south side in the Flathead National Forest. Great Northern, due south of our put-in, rises to 8,705 feet, and Nyack rises to 7,750 feet. But though we pass several creeks flowing off these mountains, we get only occasional glimpses of them when a view opens through the nearer ridgeline up the valley of one of those tributary creeks. Some slopes are only splotched with snow. Others remain completely white. Across the river, Mount Stimson guards the way into Glacier National Park and pours its melting snows down into Nyack Creek, a river that is closed to fishing to protect bull trout. Seeing the waters where bull trout still thrive is another reason for my visit here.

At 11:00 a.m. either the river flips a switch from off to on or else we just start fishing different types of water. As we approach a bend in the river, I cast toward the gravel shelf and let my pair of dry flies drift over the edge. As they float over the darker green water I see the slow rise and take of a twelve-inch cutthroat. I lead this fish into Blake's net and snap a quick photo. It is a brightly colored fish. We release it, and not five minutes later I have another one on. For the next two hours both Rob and I have steady action on the soft water behind gravel bars, off shelfs, and on inside bends. We also find hungry fish in the pools and confluence water where quiet side channels and braids or inlet creeks flow in. The current is slower here, and I suspect the water is a little warmer. They also harbor deeper pools. Most of the fish we land are ten to twelve inches but we catch a couple of fifteen-inch fish also. In one hundred-yard stretch of soft water behind a gravel bar we land four between us.

Though we cast to plenty of enticing water around log jams as we drift past, these spots remain unproductive. Still, every time we pass a log jam I cast behind it expectantly. I also keep my eye out for any signs of hatches. They are both sporadic and varied through the day. We spot a few stoneflies and a few different mayflies, but nothing thick and nothing that triggers rising fish. Still, despite the lack of visible surface action, after one brief morning period when Rob fished a wet-dry dropper combo, for the rest of the day we both fish two dry flies, and we have no reason to change.

It's hard to leave the river when the fishing is so good, but we're all getting hungry. We pull up onto a gravel bar and the guides lay out a luxurious lunch in the shade. It is quiet. The steady gentle hum of the river and the higher whistles of songbirds form our soundtrack—a variation of the theme I have been enjoying for three weeks now.

The scene isn't entirely bliss, however. For the first portion of the float, the river ran close to a road and railway. Though the riparian corridor of trees shielded our view of both asphalt road and steel track, in a strange juxtaposition to the surrounding wilderness I heard a steady succession of trains pass by. Since the locomotives were only brief (though frequent) interruptions to the soundtrack, and every place I looked I saw gorgeous water or stunning peaks, I didn't think much of it. In late morning the river had turned away from the tracks and it grew even more remote and pristine. So I am surprised when Mark mentions that the Middle Fork was listed as one of ten most endangered rivers in the country. I ask why. It's the trains, he explains. They carry oil. Though they haven't yet had a major spill, there have been numerous de-railings and avalanches along this portion of track.

The Middle Fork of the Flathead is one of the most important headwaters of the Columbia River system. A spill would have devastating ecological impact not just on the South Fork, but potentially for a long way downriver. What are the possible solutions, I ask. Mark acknowledges that re-locating the tracks would be much too expensive, and so it simply won't happen. However, there is pressure on the rail companies to replace old cars with technologically advanced cars offering extra spill protection. Conservation groups are hoping to keep that pressure up.

After lunch we get into our rafts again. I forget trains. The temperature is in the mid 80s, the warmest it has been in a week. It's great to be floating with a light breeze blowing over the cold water. I keep myself slathered in sunscreen, and wear a hat and neck Buff all day.

We have an afternoon of continued good fishing. Most of the fish I land are distinctive cutthroat, but some have coloration and spot patterns suggesting hybridization with non-native rainbow trout. Whereas a cutthroat trout has few spots below its lateral line, a rainbow trout may have many;

it's one of the telltale signs of the species difference. One of the larger fish looks all rainbow; it has no red slash on the throat, and lots of spots on its lower half. Glacier National Park still offers some of the most important waters in the country where native Westslope cutthroat trout are protected, but the presence of invasive fish in these border rivers is another threat. I know from biologists that hybridized fish are less well adapted. Offspring don't survive as well.

All of this is in the back of my mind as I enjoy the surroundings and the beauty of the fish in one of the best cutthroat trout waters I've fished. I've landed a couple in the sixteen to eighteen-inch range. Songbirds continue to sing to us from the shore. We pass a spot where bull trout are known to hang out, but we don't see any. We do watch a pair of osprey feeding over the main current and up one side channel, and then hanging out on a dead tree up the hill by the river. We fish as we drift. We anchor at likely spots. We occasionally pull up on the gravel and fish from the shore. All three are productive at times.

Finally, we approach the take-out point, where the combined waters of Mocassin and Deerlick Creeks flow into the Middle Fork. There are several fish rising in the seam at the confluence. I cast to them, and get some strikes. I hook one fish, but instead of bringing it to the boat I execute a perfect long-distance release. Finally, we have run out of time. Blake starts to paddle up the deep slow current of the inlet creek. I cast backward toward the rising fish, but we are quickly out of casting range. I reel in my fly, but keep my rod in hand.

For a hundred yards or so, the water is over-my-head deep. Still, it is clear, and there is no noticeable current to blur my vision. I study the silty bottom. I don't really expect to see a fish, but there is always some wishful thinking. We've gone up and around the first bend when, to my amazement, we see a huge cutthroat cruising the silty bottom of the deep slow-moving channel. It's the biggest fish we've seen all day. With my heart thumping, I anticipate where the fish is heading and lay my flies gently on the water fifteen feet in front of it.

Blake sees my cast and tells me this fish has already been spooked by the raft in this clear water and won't take a fly. I consider this, and think that he is almost certainly right. Still, I'd made a really nice cast. I leave my fly on the water anyway, and mend the line to avoid drag. A few seconds after the words are out of Blake's mouth we see the fish turn and start upward. Improbably, it is headed straight toward my fly. An eternity of five to six seconds passes as the fish covers a dozen feet in a leisurely deliberate rise. In the clear water, it has plenty of time to examine its food. I expect it to take a closer look at the meal, notice the artificial appearance, and then turn away. Instead the big cutthroat puts its lips to my fly and sips in.

Two minutes later we net an eighteen-inch cutthroat. It is a bright pink and green female with a red slash on the jaw indicating at least some cutthroat ancestry. We release her and watch her swim off into the deep. I'm almost ready to get out of the boat and head back to the artist-in-residence cabin to write more. I'm feeling ready to get back home to Vermont, my community, my family. But I'm also wondering how and when I'll get back to this spot—and hoping they'll get the train thing figured out soon.

When I'll get back to the Middle Fork turns out to be the afternoon just two days later. How I get back is by driving my rental car. I have no drift boat, so I will need to in a place I can wade. I park in a pull-off near where the river turns away from the railroad track, not far upstream from where we ate our lunch. I work the shoreline downstream. I land one trout in a side channel. I hook and land couple more against the bank in the main stem of the river in pools behind fallen trees. I cast again to a likely patch of soft water in another side channel. An adrenaline-producing swirl in the water precedes a big fish striking my fly which precedes my tippet breaking which precedes a deep sigh.

Not long after that I land the biggest fish of the day. It looks like pure rainbow, with no cutthroat slash, and lots of spots below the lateral line. I hike back to my car and drive down to another tributary where I fish my way down to the river mouth and back. The water is slower deeper, and siltier. To my eyes, it looks much less like trout habitat than the gravel-bottomed main stem of the Middle Fork, or even than portions of McDonald Creek. But what do I know? I land another big fish, then I hook six more and land four of them in a short time.

Someday I want to return and head thirty or more miles up the Middle Fork into the Great Bear Wilderness for a multi-day camping and fishing trip. But winter snow keeps it inaccessible until July. For now I'm content with the experiences I've had, even as they wind to an end.

Hike to Hidden Lake

Friday, June 30

My alarm goes off at 3:40 a.m. to wake me on the last day of June, the last full day of my residency in Glacier National Park. Despite how groggy I feel, I am far too excited about the day to give into the temptation to turn off the alarm and roll back over. To make an efficient morning, I've already laid out my gear for the day. While the coffee percolates, I get dressed and eat a quick bowl of cereal. The coffee goes into a thermos, and I'm heading out to the car by 4:00 a.m.

By 4:15 a.m., as I drive past the Avalanche trailhead parking area for the first time, the sky is already light enough to silhouette the park's iconic peaks. I drive along the river, and then up the lower part of the famous Going-to-the-Sun Road and around the famous Loop, where I had turned around on my bike excursion ten days earlier. Today I keep going. The road seems very narrow. On my right is a railing and sheer drop-off. On my left, the road is bounded by a jagged rock face. I think it is a one-lane road that somebody has painted a stripe down as a joke. Fortunately, I have it to myself in the pre-dawn. I can let my left tire stray over that line. However, the thought of driving back with cars approaching in the opposite direction makes me nervous. I wish I could enjoy the view to my right.

I arrive at the top around 4:45 a.m., pass the sign marking the Continental Divide at Logan Pass, and almost at once turn right into the welcome center's parking lot. In a few hours, this lot will be packed, and hopeful visitors unable to find a spot will have to turn around in disappointment. However I have the entire lot to myself for several minutes. Though sunrise is still more than half an hour away, the sky has lightened considerably. I'm torn between photographing and filming the eastern side looking into the rising sun, or walking back over the lip to the west and watching the Mc-Donald Valley slowly illuminate as the sun comes up behind me. I take a few photos looking west, but I choose the former.

As I get out of my car and walk to the lower end of the empty parking lot with video camera, camera, and tripod, I am surprised by how loud the soundtrack of the songbirds is, even up here at the very edge of the tree line, where much of the ground is still under snow. I hear thrushes and song sparrows singing from the bushes and from low shrubby spruce trees that surround the lot. I go to where the song is the loudest and set up my video camera, and start it rolling for a time lapse of the rising sun. With my thermos of hot coffee in one hand and my DSLR around my neck, I alternately stroll along the edge of the lot looking for birds, or sit still and watch them come to me.

A few other cars roll through in the dark, between 5:00 a.m. and 6:00 a.m. People step out for quick photos and move on. One other photographer—he identifies himself as being from Los Angeles and before that from the Philippines—sets up near me for a few minutes. I recognize him from Avalanche Lake the previous night where he was filming dippers in the waterfalls at dusk. We chat a bit. He is looking for a particular bird, I think. He suddenly packs up quickly and races across the parking lot to try someplace different. I spend three hours standing at the lower end of the lot enjoying the "moment". I'd like to see the iconic goats or sheep, but I don't. I do delight in the alpenglow on the peaks around me as the light slowly appears on them and then moves down their slopes. I delight in the time to be quiet. My soul is at rest. I don't need to rush or go anywhere. Songbirds sing, as though to me alone. I still don't know what they all are, though I've now come to learn a few of them by sound. There are robins, of course. They are everywhere in the park, it seems. I see them and hear them here, too. I've also learned the simple almost unnatural whistle of the Varied Thrush—a bird I thought was a bear whistle when I first heard it in the woods by Upper McDonald Creek. And a song sparrow is singing somewhere nearby. There are other birds also, more beautiful and melodic, and their songs fill this place though I catch only glimpses of them. Then a song sparrow lands on a tree close by and begins to sing, while framed perfectly against a light sky. I get one of my two favorite bird photos of the month of the joyful vocalist singing his soul out.

I also see a vole scurrying across open ground and then back into his hole. The sight of the vole makes me think about the rare and endangered Meltwater Stoneflies that live in Lunch Creek that flows off the melting snow and ice of the peak right in front of me. I wonder what the voles and other insectivore birds will do when the glaciers are gone, and the stoneflies with them.

By 8:00 a.m., a dozen or more cars have come into the lot. I put my video camera and empty coffee thermos back in the rental pickup and grab my day pack. It's time to hike into Hidden Lake. I am half-hoping to be the first one there. I'm also half-hoping to find somebody to hike with, because I know that the outlet of the lake is a regular hangout for bears. I'm also not sure I'll even get to the lake, since I heard the evening before that it was still almost completely iced

over. Since it isn't that much higher than Avalanche Lake, and sits in the same part of the park with their outlet streams flowing together, that surprises me. I don't doubt the news, however.

I get a long drink of water at the fountain, then start up the trail from behind the visitor center. I am not the first one. I can see a few hikers in the distance ahead of me. Above the timberline it is easy to see people. Somebody just a few dozen yards ahead has skis on his back. For the most part, the hike across the snow isn't bad. I have my wading staff as a hiking stick. The snow is hard packed from the cold night and a bit slick in places. Though I am in good hiking boots, at times I wish for crampons. I press on. If I reach a steep slope that seems too slippery, I will turn around. It should be easier going in the afternoon when the snow softens under the midday sun.

In about half an hour I approach the continental divide. There is no sign marking it, but I pass a shallow pond mirroring the surrounding peaks. Water flows into it from melting snow, and exits eastward down into the valley. This water will eventually make it to St. Mary Lake and on to the Hudson Bay. I cross a slight rise, and in a few hundred yards come upon another stream, this one clearly flowing westward down into a new valley. Eventually it will flow into Upper McDonald Creek, via Hidden Lake and Avalanche Creek. I am back in the watershed of the Columbia River and Pacific Ocean.

Soon I stand at Hidden Lake Overlook. A view of a distant Lake McDonald opens up through a narrow gap. Much closer and steeper down, I see Hidden Lake. It is, indeed, still covered in ice, except for a small stretch of open blue water against the far northern shore that gets more light. As I take photos of the vista opening westward before me—still in the morning shadows of the tall peaks—I notice another pair of hikers taking photos in the other direction. I look back. A half dozen mountain goats stand silhouetted atop a ledge to my south. Iconic creatures of this area, and in an iconic pose. One of them stands on the side of a steep slope a hundred feet below the others. I photograph them backlit by the morning sky. I also almost step on a big marmot, standing near the bushes by the trail. I take photos of him also.

Then I look down at my destination. I think again of how this lake is still mostly iced in on the last day of June. I look at the trail ahead. I will have to cross a steep slope covered in snow. But farther ahead, before it descends down to the lake, I get glimpses of the trail breaking clear of the snow before beginning the descent and switchbacks. After some water and a snack bar, I continue on. It's my last day. If I don't make it to Hidden Lake, I'm sure I will regret my decision later.

Soon, I am leaving the other hikers behind. There are no footprints in the snow. I am the first to pass this way today. I move slowly across the slope, taking care to kick my hiking shoes hard into the snow at an angle to make a solid hold for my foot on each step. With the extra caution, going is slow. Sometime later, I see others coming behind. I take enough photos to allow one of them to catch up. We introduce ourselves. His name is Nick. He is French, and comes from the south of France where he enjoys hiking the Pyrenees. He has just finished three years of teaching French in San Diego. We hike together. At the bottom of the slope, as we near the lakeshore, the trail drops into some thick trees. I comment about how we need to be cautious now for a different reason; this is bear territory. Nick, being perhaps wiser than I am, decides that now is time for him to hang back a little and let me go several steps ahead of him. I find myself walking onward alone, with him fifty feet behind me. I talk loudly to myself, and keep my hand on my bear spray, but I soon arrive lakeshore. I am the first one at Hidden Lake for the day.

Nick comes down the trail a minute after me. A father and his two sons follow just five minutes back. It is a little after 9:30 a.m. The water is crystal clear. It is also a blue mirror reflecting the peaks. About thirty or forty feet of open channel separates the ice from the northern shore. Beyond that, it's ice all the way across as far as I can see. Most of the lake is surrounded by cliffs that fall right to the water's edge. But as I saw on the hike down, a strip of trees lines the northeast corner where the outlet is. Once more songbirds call to me.

And trout call to me from the water. I don't see them at once, but I only have to walk fifty yards to the outlet of the lake where a small stream flows off into woods. Several trout are cruising the three-foot deep water just out into the mouth of the lake from the stream. A few more sit just where the current of the stream becomes visible. As I watch, I see a few rises.

I look behind me. Trees come right to the edge of the water. There is just enough shoreline to walk along on dry gravel, but no space for casting. I rig my L.L.Bean backpacking rod—an old 9-piece model that has long since been superseded by an 8-piece version. It has been on many trips with me and I'm comfortable with its action. I try to cast, first along the lake shore, and then in the stream mouth. The trees crowd me too closely for anything but a roll cast, and the trout are very easily spooked. Both my movement along the shore and the drag of my line across the water spooks them.

I change to sandals and wade out into the icy lake. My feet go numb almost instantly. The water cannot be much warmer than ice. Regardless of how challenging it is to cast from shore, I will not be wading long. I ask Nick to get some photos of me with my camera. He does. I get out of the water. Now all my concentration is on the trout. I cast for them, sometimes stepping out to ankle deep to cast, but quickly walking back to dry land.

I don't think I've been fishing more than five minutes when I hear a loud splashing in the river behind me. I know instinctively what that splashing is before I see the cause. My heart starts to race with anticipation as I turn to look. A grizzly splashes right up the center of the stream, not ten feet from where I had just been wading and only forty feet from where I now stand. I am sure he is hunting same thing I am, though with a very different technique. He looks at me from closer than I am comfortable. I back up several steps, but he turns and leaves the stream on the opposite bank. Only then, as the bear walks away, do I have the presence of mind to get out my camera and take photos. I watch him amble up the shoreline on ice and snow. He goes about a hundred and fifty feet and then breaks into a faster loping gait and disappears into the woods. I wonder what spooked him.

I know what spooked me. When the thumping of my heart slows somewhat, I find Nick and talk. The dad and sons shows up. We all talk. Then I go back to fishing, though even more warily. I don't spend too much time in the stream mouth after that.

For most of the rest of the morning I watch trout rising occasionally, with loud hard slaps on the surface. I see a lot of deep gold and bright red. These are not native Westslope cutthroat, but a population of Yellowstone Cutthroat stocked many years earlier. According to one biologist, they seem not to interact or interbreed with some Westlope cutthroats that live in the same lake. It is one of a couple lakes on the west side that has these non-native strain of cutthroat. The other is Grace Lake.

That's not really what I'm thinking about at the moment, though. I'm thinking about how to catch these fish. They are wary of silhouettes, and line, and movement, and seem uninterested in any dry fly I cast toward them. They are feeding on emerging insects—perhaps tiny stoneflies, or tiny mayflies. I don't see any insects, but there are heavy splashes as fish chase insects from the bottom right out of the water as they hatch. In two hours of fishing, I get only one fish to come and take a serious look at my fly. It turns away.

I think of anglers and bears. I fish dries for two hours but I get only one fish to rise to within a foot of my fly before turning away. In the crystal clear water, I try a variety of tiny dry flies, two at a time, with 6x tippet. The trout are very easily spooked by any fly landing on the surface or any movement on shore. To get that one rise I had to leave the fly on the water a long time. They want something smaller, and something coming off the bottom. By late morning when the sun finally crests the ridge, the trout stop rising and move further from the mouth of the stream. I keep watching them. They are now cruising the silty bottom and feeding there, much like the Westslope cutthroat trout in Snyder Lake. But for whatever reason—perhaps the deeper water or a greater food supply—these Hidden Lake fish are much bigger. Every now and then, one turns suddenly and darts towards something. Sometimes two dart toward the same object, invisible to me thirty or forty feet away. This confirms my guess that the fish are feeding on aquatic insects as they hatch from the bottom and swim to the surface to fly away. They are not going to bite something that lands in the water, either on the surface or sinking to the bottom. They are only going to hit something coming off the bottom and heading back toward the surface. Of course this suggests a strategy to me—one I think might work. When I go to try it, however, I find I have lost my reading glasses. I could tie on a big nymph or streamer, but without my glasses I can't tie on a tiny fly. My heart sinks and for a time I give up.

I take a lunch break, and cast the dry flies I have on but with little hope, and no success. It is futile. I walk the shoreline several times looking for my glasses, but that proves equally unsuccessful. I take a nap on the shore. When I rise it is after 1:30 p.m. After talking with a young couple, I pack to hike out. I take one more walk along the shoreline to say goodbye to the lake and the creek, and I find my glasses, with one scratch in a lens where I probably kicked them.

Now I can try my strategy. I tie on two small nymphs, a size #18 and a size #20. Though I sometimes use a #22 zebra in southern tailwaters, these are generally the smallest flies I use. They are the smallest I have with me. I have 6x tippet which is very fine. I'd use 7x, but I don't have any with me. I can barely see the flies dangling in front of my face. I can't see them at all in the water, but I can follow the movement of my little split shot as it sinks.

My feet are numb from wading in my sandals so I change back to wool socks and hiking boots for the trek home. There is one place along the shore where I can back cast at an angle, or if I am very careful I can back cast in a small gap between trees. I've lost two flies trying, but also made many successful casts.

I lay my two nymphs on the water. The fly line spooks the fish and they swim away. But I just let my flies sink to the bottom, where the water looks four to five feet deep. Then

I wait, holding my body as still as possible. After a couple minutes, the cruising trout return. I twitch my line slightly, causing my fly to lift off the bottom, at most just a few inches, but still close to the bottom silt. The biggest trout in the group follows the fly slowly. And, apparently, it likes what it sees. A moment later, it hits.

Soon I am fighting a fat Yellowstone Cutthroat, a male in bright red spawning colors as beautiful as I have seen. It is fat, and fights hard. There is one branch, about five feet long, laying on the lake bottom. No other boulders or big logs to be seen. I see that fish trying to take my line under that branch. How does it know to do that? I lift hard just in time and keep my line clear. In two minutes I land the fish.

Cutthroat are the only trout that compare in beauty with a char—such as a wild brook trout or Dolly Varden. Holding the fish by the tail with one hand, the other gently under its head, keeping the mouth and body in the cool water where it can breathe, I ask a passerby to pick up my camera and take a few photos. Then I release the fish and it swims off.

I continue to fish for another hour. Every cast takes a few minutes. With the trees behind me, it takes a few attempts to get my fly where I want it, and when I do I need to wait patiently for the spooked fish to return while my fly lies on the bottom—or I can simply cast when there are no fish around and then wait for one to come by. Often the fish don't even chase and I start again. Still, having tasted success, I persist. Somehow I hook three more. The second one is a little smaller, but just as bright. The third one—obviously the smartest—heads for the one branch the instant I hook it. And because I hooked it close to that branch, it succeeds. It swims under the little gap between branch and bottom. My lightweight tippet snaps at once and the fish swims off. The branch is right where my fly wants to drop so I make use of a gap in the trees for my backcast, making sure to keep my casts further away from the branch. The fourth trout is another big one, and though it runs for the branch I'm able to land it. I look in its mouth for the extra fly, but it isn't there. It's a different fish. I release it gently under water, and after it swims off I decide it's time—or past time—for me to begin the steep climb up the snowy hill and head back to my car.

On the way back I come upon a female goat and kid feeding at the edge of the snow. I pause to take photos. Then I drive down the famous going-to-the-sun road, reversing my morning trek in late afternoon instead of morning light. Then begins the packing for home.

Epilogue:
Colorado River Cutthroat with Kurt,
A Final Wandering Exploration

I stand on a thick tuft of grass in the midst of an alpine meadow on the bank of Cabin Creek in Colorado's Arapahoe National Forest. Mt Neva, Mt Jasper, and the iconic Devil's Thumb—all rising over 12,000 feet above sea level—line the cloudy late morning sky to the east. Evergreens, mostly pine, are colonizing the meadow. For the most part, they are still sparsely dotted, but in places they have formed thick clusters. The effort has some gains and some losses; many of the pines along the meadow's edge are brown or grey, dying or already dead, having succumbed to pine beetle infestations. The losses are more evident on the slopes around us, where dead grey patches cover about as much area as the green. Despite the ghostly skeletons of trees, however, we have come to this alpine meadow during the brief summer months when it is free of snow and the fullness of its life is evident. The abundance of life can be seen in the lush grasses and variety of white and yellow wildflowers that blanket the meadow, in the dark green of the many trees still thriving, in the constant movement of insects through the air and the grass, and in the songs of birds.

That life is especially evident, at least to me, in and around the creek where the brush and grass grow thickest. That is where my eyes focus now. At my feet, Cabin Creek meanders westward, away from the named peaks and down toward the valley and its confluence with Ranch Creek. It moves across the meadow in no particular rush, winding around the clumps of conifers, tumbling over shallow riffles, through deeper pools at the bends, and back over more riffles. The creek is shallow enough in places I can walk across it on the gravel bars without getting more than the bottoms of my hiking shoes wet. It is narrow enough in places that I could leap it—though I'm not sure I'd trust my landing on some of the undercut banks, especially on the tight bends above the deepest pools which would sink me to my knees or even the tops of my thighs were I to slip off.

I am looking at one of those undercut banks at the base of a riffle beneath an overhanging bank when the fly rod in my hand suddenly connects me to a small cutthroat trout that snatches my tan elk hair caddis fly from the surface as it floats by. Even with spider-silk-fine 6x tippet, the trout is not big enough to break my line. I lead it quickly to the near bank. Though the bright orange cut on its throat, and the lack of spots on its lower half, identifies the fish as a cut-throat, it is noticeably different from the Snake River Fine-Spotted cutthroat or the cut-bow hybrids and Yellowstone cutthroat I had caught earlier in 2016, or from the many Westslope cutthroat I would catch in Glacier National Park or the Flathead National Forest the following year. Though this little alpine trout itself is no longer than my hand, its spots are much larger than the bigger Corral Creek trout. Perhaps the most striking difference is the color. Rather than green hues with hints of the rainbow reds, this fish glows with rich earthy colors: tans and browns and golds. Its color-ation matches the mix of hues of the stones and pebbles on the shallow streambed. Perhaps a micro adaptation offering better camouflage?

My day started several hours earlier, on the opposite side of the continental divide: the east slope. It is the final full day of my 2016 summer trip to Wyoming and Montana with Yuki and Julia. Except we are no longer in Wyoming or Montana. We have come to Colorado for our last day and a half. We will spend tomorrow with professional filmmaker and Middlebury alumni Andrew Ackerman to garner some guidance and suggestions about filmmaking as we prepare to turn nearly four weeks of explorations—with several combined hours of video footage and interviews—into just a few short digital stories, edited and narrated to share on You-Tube.

Today we get to spend the day with Colorado State University fisheries biologist Kurt Fausch. Kurt meets us at our hotel in Boulder and we drive together into the mountains to the resort town of Fraser, near the Winter Park ski resort. From there we hike into the Arapahoe National Forest to one of Kurt's former study sites, where native Colorado River cutthroat trout can still be found in a few high alpine streams.

In some ways, looking for wild native Colorado River cutthroat is a fitting conclusion to our trip. We had started the month in Wyoming on La Barge Creek in a different headwater of the Colorado River, at a project working to restore that same subspecies to another of its native waters. A golden eagle—or perhaps a colonizing population of cutthroat trout in the days before the damming of the Colorado River watershed—could have followed La Barge Creek downriver into the Green River, then continued southward down the Green out of Wyoming and three quarters of the way across Utah to its confluence with the Colorado River in Canyonlands National Park. The eagle or ambitious trout could then have turned northeast and followed the Colorado River upstream out of Utah and into Colorado to the mountain town of Granby, and from there flown or swum up Fraser Creek to Winter Park. In the town of Tabernash, a colonizing population of trout might have veered a little east off Fraser Creek and headed up Ranch Creek. And from Ranch Creek, it might have taken a sharp left turn into Cabin Creek, heading northeast and then east further into the hills, where with some steep climbing and hard swimming it could have found itself in a little meadow at an elevation of 9,650 feet in what is now the Arapahoe National Forest. Ten thousand years ago that trout and its generations of progeny might also have reversed that aquatic route, connecting from Cabin Creek back down and then up into the La Barge.

Indeed, the appropriateness of a visit to that part of Colorado was for me doubly fitting—a full circle return to an important place in my own formative experience with both fly fishing and cutthroat trout. Almost four decades earlier, halfway through my teenage years, my father's work with independent bookstores had taken our family for a week to the town of Granby, near the confluence of Fraser Creek and a branch of the Colorado River. There, my father arranged a guided day of fishing for myself and my two older brothers, and I'd had my first experience fly fishing, and my first encounter with cutthroat trout. I still have vivid memories of standing in the river in my "tennies"—our guide's term for sneakers, which I wore for wading shoes since I didn't yet own waders or real wading boots. The guide stood beside us, demonstrating how to spot trout feeding in the rips, how cast a fly rod, and how to set a hook. He had the rods rigged with two dry flies: an Adams and a Hornberg. I only remembered the name of the latter fly because of the coincidental association with a moutainside fortress known as the Hornburg in the land of Rohan in J.R.R.Tolkien's *The Lord of the Rings*. On our guide's first cast, intended just to demonstrate to us what to do, he hooked and landed two fish at the same time, one on each fly. In doing so, he also simultaneously hooked two teenage anglers on the joys of fly fishing, one of them being me and the other being one of my older brothers.

Though I have been not back there in several decades, and I have no photographs of the day, I retain vivid memories of standing on the bank with my brothers and our guide, spread along a big bend where the Colorado flowed into Columbine Bay on Lake Granby, a short stretch downstream of the dam on Shadow Mountain Lake. Not another angler could be seen. I still dream about the place. I might hesitate to return now for fear of how it may have changed, or that my memories might prove false, or that it will have become yet another one of those famous trophy trout waters that now host combat fishing.

Years later I would learn that Jerry Craig, our friendly and unpretentious guide, was already a fly fishing and guiding legend, or was well on his way to becoming one at the time he took us fishing. Through our day with Jerry and the subsequent week exploring local waters on our own, in addition to the cutthroat trout, we also experienced invasive rainbow trout, brook trout, and lake trout in the mountains of Colorado. As a teenager who had grown up fishing in Maine and Massachusetts, I could confidently tell the difference between brook trout, lake trout, and rainbow trout, but I couldn't have told the difference between rainbow trout and cutthroat trout. I had no idea there were multiple distinct subspecies of cutthroat trout, and it would be decades before I learned which of those were native in which parts of the country, which were not, and why it was important.

I do remember being quite impressed walking into a shop to buy some flies, and seeing a massive lake trout trophy on the wall. My memory is that it had weighed thirty-six pounds. In awe bordering on disbelief—not just at the size and existence of such a fish, but that somebody could actually catch one—I ask the shopkeeper about it. He laughed and nodded toward our guide, indicating that it was he who had landed it, and that he'd done so on lightweight fly gear. When I later learned that non-native lake trout like that one grew so big by decimating the population of native cutthroat trout, and why its presence was ecologically so unhealthy, it still did not take away from the prowess of the angler who caught it. I would like to have found Jerry Craig at some point later in my life and let him know how he had helped instill in me a lifetime passion for fly fishing, wild trout, and the beauty of mountains and mountain rivers. But by the time I thought to do so as an adult—and the internet had made such a name-only search possible—it was too late. Seven years before my trip to Wyoming, cancer had taken Jerry Craig's life. My internet search for his name found an obituary.

The drive with Kurt proved enjoyable and informative. In some ways, I had been acquainted with him for a few years. My friend David O'Hara introduced me to him virtually. The previous year, David and I had used Kurt's beautiful book *For the Love of Rivers* as the primary text for our summer class in Alaska on rivers, trout, ecology, and narrative non-fiction nature and environmental writing. Since Yuki and Julia both took that class, they were also familiar with his writing. And Kurt had read *Downstream: Reflec-*

tions on Brook Trout, Fly Fishing, and the Waters of Appala-chia, one of the books David and I had co-authored. He'd even written a short endorsement for the back cover. We had talked on the phone and exchanged several e-mails, but until he showed up at our hotel lobby, we had never met in person. So over the first part of the day, we were all getting to know each other. Kurt told us about his family, about his early love for clean water and wild fish that came to him primarily through his mother (who hated the heat and always wanted to be in a cold lake), and about his college education in fisheries biology and ecology. He also described how he was winding down his career as a biologist and pro-fessor at Colorado State, no longer doing active field work. He was taking us to an old research site he hadn't been to in years.

Once we turned up into the mountains, escaping In-terstate 70 for a winding state highway 40, our conversation turned to our topic of the day: the past, present, and future of Colorado River Cutthroat. We stopped in town to pick up fishing licenses, and then turned east off highway 40 to head higher on progressively less-well-traveled ways, even-tually finding the forest service roads that took us to the Devil's Thumb Trailhead. Once we left the car and started up the trail on foot, the conversation became even more focused on our immediate surroundings.

Our first stop was a small water diversion dam. The little concrete edifice remains both the bane of cutthroat trout, and, in this tiny stream, its savior. The dam represents both the major problems of water diversion and stream fragmen-tation. It is also the one barrier that prevents invasive trout that had taken over the rivers down in the valley—most notably brook trout—from invading the upper portions of Cabin Creek.

Despite the fact that this little dam is just a tiny fraction of the size of the Hungry Horse Dam at the edge of the Flathead National Forest in Montana, it is tempting to make a comparison between the impact of the two. Both, certainly, have a fragmenting impact on their respective waters while also providing an obstacle to invasive migrations. Yet there are significant differences between the conservation issues and challenges for cutthroat trout in the northern Rockies and those in the more southerly Rockies. Some of these differences came up in our conversation. In broad terms, certainly, the same ecological threats to native cutthroat in Montana and Wyoming can be seen in Colorado, and vice versa. Indeed, the biggest issues are common to waters nearly everywhere in the continent: invasive species, climate change, and habitat degradation due to development and resource extraction. Even the subcategories of habitat degradation are similar, including river fragmentation. But the balance and weight of those issues in Colorado are quite different than in much of Montana or Wyoming, especially in and around the national parks and national forests.

For one thing, Colorado has long been more developed. Fausch spoke of it in terms of a greater "human impact on the landscape". Dams, river channelization, loss of canopy from deforestation, and runoff from roads, parking lots, shopping malls are all more pervasive in Colorado. None of the rivers I spent time on in Wyoming in 2016, or would spend time on in Montana in 2017, were downstream of cities or major towns. None flowed past or off the slopes of ski areas.

The river habitat in the well-forested national parks and national forests to the north benefit from extensive preservation efforts. And water withdrawal is not in issue. In Colorado by contrast, water withdrawal is a major concern for river ecology. Not only is water drawn from the streams for local ski areas and towns—such as happened right there at the little concrete dam on Cabin Creek—but in many places water from the west slope is diverted in underground tunnels all the way to the east slope to feed cities like Denver and to help irrigate the plains. "We remove a lot of the flow and send the water from west to east," Fausch noted.

Colorado also has an older and more extensive history of stocking of non-native species. You could hear sadness or longing in Fausch's voice as he pointed out, "In Colorado we don't have any more big rivers that don't have non-native trout in them or that have good enough habitat." He added that there aren't really any feasible locations or opportunities to restore native fish to major watersheds in Colorado. There are no practical places to build barriers to get rid of the non-natives and restore the native fish. As a result, the few places in his state where native cutthroat still hold on are often marginal waters: creeks where the habitat is only just barely habitable year round, where brook trout are not able to successful colonize, and cutthroat populations simply cling to life until some disaster strikes. Sometimes it's only the final few hundred yards of headwater on some alpine stream. Or a place like Cabin Creek where an artificial barrier was in place soon enough to block the invasion. Fausch fears the day when somebody brings a few brook trout above that dam and sets them free in the upper portion of Cabin Creek.

Listening to his words, I thought of the headwaters of Hungry Horse Reservoir in the Flathead National Forest, and the numerous alpine lakes in Glacier National Park where native Westslope cutthroat could still be found. Even Yellowstone Lake, although the cutthroat population has been decimated by invasive lake trout, is still free of invasive rainbow trout and so the native strain of Yellowstone cutthroat is not (yet) under threat of hybridization. I think again of how important those waters are, and how important it is to protect them. Fausch notes more than once that it's much harder to restore something once it's lost than it is to protect it in the first place. He paraphrases Aldo Leopold, noting that the important principle in intelligent tinkering is to make sure you keep all the parts of the machine: every cog and wheel. Thus, as bad as a brook trout invasion would be, if some remnant native cutthroat population survived it might in theory be possible to restore them. When rainbow trout invade, and the hybridization with cutthroat trout begins, you lose one of the parts; the machine can't be rebuilt. In that area, at least, Colorado shared a concern common to some of the waters in Glacier National Park such as the North and Middle Forks of the Flathead, and the lakes reachable from those rivers.

We leave the dam and continue on up the trail, talking as we go. I record the conversation. At the meadow, Yuki sets up the video camera. Kurt talks some more, speaking to us and the camera at the same time. He speaks passionately about the importance of the meadow we sit in, and of Cabin Creek which flows through it. "Usually the [remnant] cutthroat are stuck in the high elevation, high gradient places," he tells us, describing the marginal waters where they have been pushed by invasive species. He compares it to what it would be like if a group of humans were forced to live in the Arctic, and not allowed to go to grocery stores. He then praises Cabin Creek. "Here they have a meadow with pools. It's relatively flat, with ground water upwelling that keeps them from freezing [in the winter]." It's still not ideal. The natural habitat where cutthroat would really thrive is down in the big rivers in the valley below, with miles of connected waters and a variety of habitats. But at least in this large meadow, in Cabin Creek, they have types of habitat that are lacking elsewhere, and—barring an introduction of brook trout above they dam—the population has a hope of continuing.

Thinking once again about fragmentation and marginalization, I asked how many kilometers of river a cutthroat needs or makes use of during its life cycle. Kurt acknowledge that the question is not easy and that there are lots of unknowns, and also that it will vary from river to river, watershed to watershed. Still, there are some good guidelines. "We fish biologists know some things about how small is too small. The rule of thumb is that in Colorado ten kilometers of stream is what gets you something that is good." That includes deep stable habitat needed in the water, less susceptible to catastrophic events that with climate change are now more common. "They can spawn in many places," he notes, "but overwinter habitat is critical."

The comment brings us to the topic of climate change, and yet another irony. The high elevation streams where remnant cutthroat trout populations have been pushed, and where they still survive, are not too warm. In many cases, they are below the ideal temperature. Thus the warming of water brought about by climate change could theoretically be more favorable to cutthroat trout, at least in terms of temperature. Unfortunately, climate change is likely to cause a different set of problems. For example, in places the streams will become too dry. The late summer base flow after snow melt is critical, Fausch tells us. That is certainly threatened. And as he has already noted, we can expect increasing catastrophic events as a result of climate change.

But why does it matter that the cutthroat survive at all, I ask, repeating a question I began the summer with, and which I have put to numerous biologists. I get two answers.

One is the ecological answer I have been learning about, and will continue to learn about, from all the biologists I have spoken with or will speak with. Fausch explains the answer with his own extensive research on the impacts of brook trout invasion of a native cutthroat trout stream. "After brook trout invade a stream and completely take over, they reduce the amount of aquatic insects emerging into the riparian zone by at least a third, and possibly as much as fifty-five percent. . . So what does that mean? A whole set of animals that live in the riparian zone—birds and bats and lizards and spiders and other small mammals depend on this pulse of insects that are coming out of a stream—in some cases all through the winter. [Experiments indicate] It's reducing the insects that two-thirds of the riparian birds need." In other words, Fausch explains, it's not just other species of trout that suffer from the invasive fish; it's the whole ecosystem. Add brook trout to a Rocky Mountain cutthroat trout stream and you can expect for two-thirds of the riparian birds to disappear. Add lake trout to a Rocky Mountain lake and the number of ospreys collapse by more than ninety percent.

Kurt's other answer surprises me, though. It is not a dry scientific answer. It's not a scientific answer at all. Though it is the sort of answer one might expect from a scientist who writes a book about rivers with the word "love" in the title. It is, in part, a cultural answer. It is an answer that appeals to values:

> When I think about non-native trout that we've spread around the world—brook, brown, and rainbow trout— you can go anywhere in the world and catch those fish. I can go to Japan and catch rainbow trout, and brook trout, and brown trout. I can go to Germany and catch rain-

bow trout, go to Scandinavia and catch brook trout. But the western United States is the only place you can see cutthroat trout and catch cutthroat trout. We've stocked them around the world but they haven't established any population that I know about. So If you want to see the fish that evolved in these streams for the last 10,000 years or so—and in Montana and Wyoming it might be 70,000 to a million years—if you want to see those fish, it's the only place you're going to see them. So . . . one reason to [care] is that it's the only place they'll ever be. And it's very difficult to restore them once they're gone.

Listening to Fausch's words, I think back two weeks to the day I spent in the Shoshone National Forest northwest of Cody with the USFS fisheries biologist Shawn Anderson. I think of Shawn's obvious delight and passion as we sat in the USFS office in Cody while he showed us a game camera film of grizzly bears feeding on spawning cutthroat trout in a small stream flowing through the national forests.

I also think of the day-long field trip we took with Anderson after watching that film, driving into the national forest to visit two different rivers with ongoing or hoped-for cutthroat projects. Both rivers were tributaries of the Clark's Fork of the Yellowstone, a watershed in which Yellowstone cutthroat were native. The stretch of one of those rivers we visited was above a natural waterfall barrier, which prior to the settling of Euro-Americans held no native trout of any species. Decades ago, somebody had stocked brook trout there. The USFS and Wyoming Game and Fish had removed those brook trout a few years earlier, and replaced them with Yellowstone cutthroat—the species indigenous to the local watershed, though not to that particular upstream portion of that river. It was a project Anderson might have been wary of in other waters where there were no native trout. Just as the introduction of brook trout will alter the ecosystem of a native cutthroat trout stream as it displaced and devastated the cutthroat population, so too will introduction of cutthroat into a stream that had no indigenous trout also alter the ecosystem in ways that may devastate populations of invertebrates or salamanders, with effects rippling out into the surrounding forest.

But in the case of this particular river, the damage had already been done decades ago by brook trout. The replacement of those brook trout with cutthroat provided one refuge above an impassable barrier where cutthroat might survive and even thrive: a gene pool that might be critical later, if and when other cutthroat trout streams are lost. A few rivers like this could mean the survival of a species. We walked along the river, first by the shore where I took photos and noticed a tremendous amount of invertebrate life, and then across a grassy hillside with a great view of the valley upriver of where we stood. I resisted the urge to cross the meadow down to the river and fish.

We then visited another stream that still had invasive brook trout. A potential downstream barrier made it a great candidate to remove those invasive trout and restore the native cutthroat. The obstacles to the project were neither scientific nor technological; they were political. Influential local landowners didn't want the native fish restored. They wanted their brook trout. "Some anglers just want to catch the fish they want to catch where and when they want to catch them," Shawn explained. They may like rainbow trout better than cutthroat, for whatever reason. And they want to continue to catch them in their favorite river. Or maybe they caught brook trout in the river when they were a kid, and they want to keep catching brook trout. They don't care if there are wild cutthroat or not. They don't want their favorite fish taken away. Some of these land owners along streams with proposed restoration projects have often been particularly vocal in their objections to change.

There is other opposition as well, and sometimes it comes from those who care deeply about issues of conservation. Tim Wade has been guiding on the North Fork of the Shoshone River near Cody Wyoming for some four decades. His North Fork Anglers, a fly shop and guide service, has been the face of trout fishing on the river. I remember fishing it with him back in 2004, and being as impressed with his care for the river as with his skill as a guide as he somehow got me onto a couple big browns even after a thunderstorm had ripped through the valley turning the water into a mocha latte with at most fourteen inches of visibility. Two days after my field trip with Shawn Anderson, I was able to spend another day with Tim farther up the North Fork in the National Forest.

The North Fork drainage still holds some cutthroat trout especially in some of the higher stretches and tributaries, Tim told us. The river hadn't been stocked with hatchery fish for years. It is a hodgepodge of trout species, wild and self-sustaining, but not native. In addition to remnants of its once-native cutthroat population, it also holds a thriving, reproducing population of strong, fat, hard-fighting rainbow trout. As happens in nearly all rivers with the two species, the cutthroat and rainbows have hybridized, and so the North Fork also holds cut-bows. It is unlikely that any of the cutthroat found in the river are still a pure native strain. The river also holds a small population of wild brown trout, and certain portions and tributaries also hold brook trout. Fat ones. Trophy-sized lake trout swim in the Buffalo Bill Cody Reservoir at the lower end of the river, and attract a significant number of lake anglers. Those lake trout are also famous for swimming upriver into the North Fork and feasting on cutthroat and other trout, which is how they get to be trophy sized. The North Fork is managed as a wild fishery and it is a fantastic one.

Although the lower dozen miles of the river just above the reservoir flows through private land, the upper portion flows through and drains the Shoshone National Forest. This is a wild and scenic area with one of the densest populations of grizzly bears outside of Alaska and Yellowstone. Many of its small tributaries flow through roadless tracks of the national forest and are loaded with trout. Would-be anglers are warned not to try to pursue them without a can of bear spray and lots of safety precautions.

With his long history on the North Fork, Tim Wade knows the river perhaps as well as anybody. It is his livelihood to know it. And he cares about it. He wants to see the river remain healthy—not only for anglers and clients, but for the grizzlies and the other wildlife that live along the river. If you go fishing with him, he will insist not only on a catch-and-release ethic, but on barbless hooks to make it easy to release the fish unharmed. He will tell his clients not to take fish out of the water for prolonged photos. And he has them use heavy enough line to fight the fish quickly so as not to tire them.

If you fish with him, or meet with him in the shop, he will talk with you about the history on the river, and the changes he has seen, like the impact of the big forest fires three decades ago. He will also talk, with some poignancy, about the impact of development and climate change. How the increase in houses along the river, and driveways over feeder creeks, have increased silt and pollution and damaged the ecosystem. Along with the impact on water quality, he has seen the impact of increased fishing pressure especially from those who don't a practice catch-and-release ethic. He wants to river to hold a wild trout population and decries the fill-the-freezer mentality. He'd like to see the current conservation rules enforced more actively.

He is also skeptical of attempts to restore native cutthroat to waters where they have already been displaced. Such attempts are simply not possible, he argues, in any practical sense.

We finish our interview with Kurt Fausch. Yuki turns off the video camera. Now I take out my fly rod and rig it. Kurt takes out a Tenkara rod. The Tenkara technique, which was developed in small mountain streams in Japan, is perfect for this little meandering alpine creek. The name means "*fishing* from heaven", or "*fishing* from the skies". At nearly 10,000 feet in elevation, it feels like we are in the skies. Indeed, the beauty of the place is heavenly.

The rod also seems fitting for Kurt, much of whose research on trout—including the impact of invasive species on riparian spiders and birds—was inspired by collaborative work he did in Japan with the late Shigeru Nakano. Julia and Yuki stay with Kurt and watch him use his Tenkara rod. I wander off alone making my way upstream across the meadow looking for my own likely spots to cast my little elk hair caddis. Casting blindly to a pool, I find one cutthroat which snatches my fly before I even see it. When I try to get a photo, it shoots out of my hand before I can capture the shot. I move on. Because I'm as interested in watching a fish as catching one, I move slowly and study the water as I go. The next one I see finning in the current is a mere flickering shadow against the gravel that doesn't materialize into a fish until I stare at it for several seconds.

Finally I flick my caddis fly upstream, and watch it suck my fly in as it floats past. I briefly hold my second wild cutthroat, no longer than my hand, no longer than the first one. But each is a wonder and delight to hold briefly in the cool water. I get a photo of the second one with my cell phone. This turns out to be fortunate, because when I return to find the others, my students make me produce the photo as proof of the catch. Kurt had also managed, with the aid of his Tenkara rod, to show a beautiful Colorado River cutthroat to the students.

As we turn to hike back down to the car, a cow and calf moose pair appears at the end of the meadow. The big cow is dark, dark brown, almost black. The calf is a soft light brown. We delay our departure long enough to watch them both from a safe distance. It's hard to leave. Hard for Julia and Yuki to walk away from the moose. Harder for me to walk away from an alpine creek with wild cutthroat—both a remnant of, and a hope for, its species.

WORKS CITED

Behnke, Robert J. *Trout and Salmon of North America*. New York: The Free Press, 2002.

Berry, Wendell. "A Native Hill." In *The Hudson Review*, 21:4 (Winter, 1968-1969): pp. 601-634.

Dickerson, Matthew. "The Clearcut, the Cutthroat, and the Cascade Effect." In *The Written River* 5:2 (Winter, 2015) 6-9.

Dillard, Annie. *Pilgrim at Tinker Creek* (in *Three by Annie Dillard*). New York: HarperPerennial, 1990.

Fausch, Kurt D. *For the Love of Rivers: A Scientist's Journey*. Corvallis: Oregon State University Press, 2015.

Kimmerer, Robin Wall. Braiding Sweetgrass. Minneapolis: Milkweed Editions, 2013.

Loxterman, Janet L. and Ernest R. Keeley. "Watershed boundaries and geographic isolation: patterns of diversification in cutthroat trout from western North America." In *Evolutionary Biology* 12:38 (2012). https://bmcevolbiol. biomedcentral.com/articles/10.1186/1471-2148-12-38 accessed 11/17/2020.

Metcalf, J.L., S.L. Stowell, C.M. Kennedy, K.B. Rogers, D. Mcdonald, J. Epp, K. Keepers, A. Cooper, J.J. Austin, and A.P. Martin. "Historical stocking data and 19th century DNA reveal human-induced changes to native diversity and distribution of cutthroat trout." *Molecular Ecology* 2012.

http://ppctu.org/wp-content/uploads/2015/11/mec12028_
Metcalf_etal_2012.pdf accessed 1/18/2020.

O'Hara, David and Matthew Dickerson, *Downstream: Reflections on Brook Trout, Fly Fishing, and the Waters of Appalachia*. Eugene: Cascade Press, 2014.

Tolkien, J.R.R. "On Fairy-Stories." In Tree and Leaf. Boston: Houghton Mifflin Company, 1989.

Wohlleben, Peter. *The Hidden Life of Trees: What They Feel, How They Communicate*. Vancouver: Greystone Books, 2015.

About the Author

Matthew Dickerson began writing about fishing and outdoor sports in 1997 when he accepted an invitation to pen an outdoors column for his local newspaper, the *Addison Independent*. More than two decades later, his column is still in print and has won a *New England Newspaper and Press Association* (NENPA) award for the best sports column of the year. The column (which runs every other week) is a modest side gig from his full-time job teaching at Middlebury College and his ongoing career as a fiction writer and essayist/critic.

Dickerson soon branched out from newspapers and began writing for various fly-fishing and outdoor magazines, including print publications such as *The Drake, Eastern Fly Fishing, Northwest Fly Fishing, American Fly Fishing,* and *Backcountry Journal,* and for online publications including *Fly Fishing International* (FFIMAGAZINE.COM) and Yankee Magazine's NEWENGLAND.COM. His essays of creative narrative non-fiction in the nature writing and environmental genres have appeared in journals such as *Written River, Books and Culture, Creation Care, The Other Journal,* and *Christian History Magazine.*

Dickerson eventually wove those two threads of writing—the more explicitly environmental or ecological thread and the outdoors and fly-fishing thread—together in several books. In 2012, he and his friend David O'Hara were awarded the *Spring Creek Project Environmental Nonfiction Writing Residence* at Oregon State University's Cabin at Shotpouch Creek. The result of that residency was Dickerson's first book-length collection of creative non-fiction, a collaboration with O'Hara titled *Downstream: Reflections on Brook Trout, Fly Fishing, and the Waters of Appalachia* (Cascade Press, 2014). The residency also led indirectly to the *Heartstreams* series published by Wings Press of San Antonio. The present volume is the third in that series. The first two were *Trout in the Desert: on Fly Fishing, Human Habits, and the Cold Waters of the Arid Southwest* (Wings Press, 2015) and *A Tale of Three Rivers: of Wooly Buggers, Bowling Balls, Cigarette Butts and the Future of Appalachian Brook Trout* (Wings Press, 2018).

After the Spring Creek Project residence, Dickerson was selected by Glacier National Park as their June, 2017 Artist-in-Residence and by Acadia National Park as a May, 2018 Artist-in-Residence. Those residencies, along with multiple trips to The Farm Lodge in Alaska, led to the publication of *The Voices of Rivers: Reflections on Places Wild and Almost Wild* (Homebound Publications, 2019) and to the volume in hand, *A Fine-Spotted Trout on Corral Creek: On the Cutthroat Competition of Native Trout in the Northern Rockies* (Wings Press, 2021).

Dickerson's first novel was a work of medieval historical fiction, *The Finnsburg Encounter* (Crossway Books, 1991). That novel—inspired by Dickerson's graduate study of Old English Language and Literature and the works of J.R.R. Tolkien—was later picked up for publication in German translation as *Licht über Friesland*. More than a decade later, he published a sequel entitled *The Rood and the Torc: The Song of Kristinge, Son of Finn* (Wings Press, 2014.)

Just a year later, Dickerson's first fantasy novel came into print. *The Gifted*, the first of three-volume work collectively titled *The Daegmon War* was published in 2015 by AMG. Drastic changes at this publisher led Dickerson to take control of the series and self-publish the second and third volumes of the series: *The Betrayed* and *Illengond*.

Dickerson's study of medieval and fantasy literature also led to several books and book chapters in the area of literary studies. Several of these also drew upon Dickerson's interest in and study of environmental literature. These works included a study of the theological and moral aspects of Tolkien's writings, *Following Gandalf: Epic Battles and Moral Victory in the Lord of the Rings* (a finalist for the year's Mythopoeic Society award for best work of scholarship) and a later revised and expanded version titled *A Hobbit Journey: Discovering the Enchantment of J.R.R. Tolkien's Middle-earth*. This book was followed by *Ents, Elves, and Eriador: The Environmental Vision of J.R.R. Tolkien* (with Jonathan Evans), *From Homer to Harry Potter: A Handbook on Myth and Fantasy* (with David O'Hara), and *Narnia and the Fields of Arbol: the Environmental Vision of C.S. Lewis* (also with David O'Hara).

Dickerson's other published works include a biography of the late singer-songwriter Mark Heard, *Hammers and Nails: the Life and Music of Mark Heard*; a work on the philosophy of mind, computing, and religion, *The Mind and the Machine: what it Means to be Human and Why it Matters*, and a work of spiritual theology, *Disciple Making in a Culture of Power, Comfort and Fear*.

Dickerson is a member of the *Chrysostom Society* and the *Outdoor Writers Association of America* (OWAA). He still teaches at Middlebury College (Vermont) where he spent over ten years directing (and many more years teaching at or on the steering committee for) the *New England Young Writers' Conference* at Breadloaf. He is currently working on two projects: a collection of essays about trout and rivers in Alaska and a new work of fantasy fiction.

Colophon

This first edition of *A Fine-Spotted Trout on Corral Creek*, by Matthew Dickerson, has been printed on 60 pound "natural" paper containing a percentage of recycled fiber. Titles have been set in Nueva Standard type, the text in Adobe Caslon type. This book was designed by Bryce Milligan.

Wings Press titles are distributed to the trade by the
Independent Publishers Group
www.ipgbook.com
and in Europe by Gazelle
www.gazellebookservices.co.uk

Also available as an ebook.